COUNTRY INNS
OF THE FAR WEST:
CALIFORNIA

OTHER BOOKS IN THE COUNTRY INNS SERIES

COUNTRY INNS OF THE FAR WEST: CALIFORNIA

JACQUELINE KILLEEN

ROY KILLEEN
Illustrations

101 PRODUCTIONS
San Francisco

COVER DRAWING: El Encanto Hotel, Santa Barbara, Drawing by Roy Killeen, color rendering by Lynne O'Neil.

MAPS: Lynne O'Neil

Some of the drawings in this book have been reproduced from the inns' brochures with the permission of the inns, and are credited to the following artists: The Britt House, page 6, Robert Hostick; The Venice Beach House, page 21, Hipple-Sommerville Assoc.; Salisbury House, page 22, Mimi Stuart; The Glenborough Inn, page 39, Donna Medley; Bath Street Inn, page 42, James Zimmerman; Union Hotel, page 47, Scott Gorsline; Rose Victorian Inn, page 49, Judith Andresen; The Jabberwock, page 63, Gloria Bottaro; The Stonehouse Inn, page 70, Nancy Taylor; Babbling Brook Inn, page 83, Bob Shockley; Hermitage House, page 91, T. Anna Binkley; Spreckels Mansion, page 100, James Dowlen; Petite Auberge, page 110, Nancy Taylor; Blackthorne Inn, page 122, Tony Lofting; Gramma's Bed and Breakfast Inn, page 124, Steven Lustig; Captain Dillingham's Inn, page 126, R. Norton; The Briggs House, page 133, Lily Toppenberg; Coloma Country Inn, page 135, Joanne Tepper; The Hanford House, page 145, Larry Schuman; The Haydon House, page 195, George Espinosa; Vintners Inn, page 197, Dan Obenchain; Ridenhour Ranch House Inn, page 199; Mendocino Village Inn, page 220, Judy Brown; Pudding Creek Inn, page 225, Susan Flanduz; Toll House Inn, page 227; Marguerite Slutkin, M&M Graphics.

Printed and bound in the United States of America. Distributed to the book trade in the United States by The Macmillan Publishing Company, New York, and in Canada by Raincoast Books, Vancouver.

Published by 101 Productions
834 Mission Street
San Francisco, California 94103

Library of Congress Cataloging in Publication Data

Killeen, Jacqueline.
    Country inns of the Far West—California.
    Includes index.
    1. Hotels, taverns, etc.--California--Directories.
I. Killeen, Roy.   II. Title.
TX907.K484 1987   646'.9479401   86-21735
ISBN 0-89286-268-8

Country inns of the Far West--California.

CONTENTS

INTRODUCTION

Ten years ago, when we published the first edition of *Country Inns of the Far West,* we listed only fifty-eight inns from the Mexican border to Vancouver Island. And these were not easy to find. There were no books on the subject, and the out-of-the-way places we sought were not included in general travel guides. We took to the road, searching small towns, back roads and even big cities for the quintessential country inn. In that early book, as in this edition, we included a mix of hostelries, new and old: small hotels, lodges, inns, resorts and a phenomenon new to the West in the 1970s—the English-style bed and breakfast inn.

Though only a decade ago, those days seem a century away. By 1983 the number of inns on the West Coast had grown so dramatically that we split the book into California and Pacific Northwest editions. By 1987 it seemed that almost every town in California had a so-called B&B. Meanwhile bookstore shelves bulged with bed-and-breakfast directories, some compiled by writers who never ventured beyond their word processors. (A notable exception is the thoroughly researched and highly selective *Bed & Breakfast: California* by Linda Kay Bristow.)

Country Inns of the Far West, however, is not and never was a book primarily about B&Bs. We also think the cutesy inn of the 1970s—with shared baths and a motherly innkeeper hovering over you with a cup of tea—is passé. Today's sophisticated traveler is more demanding than the vacationer of a decade ago, placing more value upon comfort than quaintness. And today's smart innkeepers are delivering the goods.

Thus, in this edition of the book, we are including only the very best of the B&Bs, places that offer more than bed and croissants alone: exceptional decor and service along with, perhaps, magnificent views or an unusual site, whirlpool baths or a spa, a sumptuous breakfast or— another British tradition that's caught on in the America of the 1980s— high tea.

Another significant 1980s trend is the emergence of the small luxury hotel or resort, a romantic spot that is often a self-contained destination in itself. We have included several such places in this book. Rates there are usually expensive, but a few days' visit might bring a lifetime of memories.

Romance is not the only reason for patronizing country inns. Many cater to lovers of sports and nature; we have included the best of these places, too. Some welcome the entire family; others provide a haven away from home and special services for the business traveler. Businesses are discovering that the relaxing ambience of a country inn is ideal for small conferences, and we have annotated those places that have appropriate facilities. In short, we have tried to include a range of inns for all tastes, for those who seek privacy and for those who like to socialize, for those who want a whirlwind of activity and for those who prefer to do nothing.

In compiling this tenth-anniversary edition of *Country Inns of the Far West,* as with previous editions, we hit the road. We traveled several thousand miles to visit personally every new hostelry included in the book, along with many older ones and numerous other places whose pretty brochures belied not-so-attractive accommodations. The bottom-line question, as always, was, would we want to stay here? Would you? We hope you enjoy this edition of *Country Inns of the Far West* as much as we have enjoyed researching it for you.

—Jacqueline and Roy Killeen

RULES OF THE INN

Rates Due to price fluctuations, specific rates are not quoted in this book. Instead we have classified the rates for two people sharing a room as follows: under $60, inexpensive; $60–$85, moderate; $85–$125, expensive; over $125, very expensive. When dinner is included in the price, we have adjusted the scale to reflect this. These price classifications were based upon rates at the time of publication and are subject to change. Many inns also have lower off-season and midweek rates, as well as group rates for business conferences. Inquire.

Reservations, Deposits, Cancellations and Refunds Reservations are advised, especially during peak travel periods. On holidays and weekends, inns are often booked for months in advance. Most establishments require a deposit of at least one night's lodging; many require a minimum stay of two nights on the weekends. In most cases your deposit will not be refunded if you cancel at the last minute; sometimes even a week's notice is required. Call or write in advance to ask about the current requirements, rates and refund policies.

Tipping In the larger inns, where you are presented your check at the end of each meal, tip as you would in any hotel or restaurant. In the smaller inns, where the owner does the cooking and serving, you are not required to tip. In fact, most innkeepers will not accept tips, and some would be insulted. If you wish to express your appreciation, send flowers or leave some wine as you would in a friend's home. You should, however, compensate the innkeeper's helpers. At the end of your stay, ask the innkeeper for advice in handling this.

No-Smoking Policies Many of the smaller inns do not allow smoking within the building, although in most cases guests are free to smoke outdoors on porches, patios or in the gardens. These inns have adopted this policy for important reasons: consideration of other guests and fear of fire or damage to priceless antiques.

Facilities for the Handicapped Wheelchair access means only that one or more rooms may be reached with no stairs from a parking area. Fully equipped for the handicapped means wheelchair access, plus extra-wide doors, and bathrooms specially designed with grab bars and other safety features as prescribed by local building codes, which vary. It is advisable to inquire about your particular needs when making reservations.

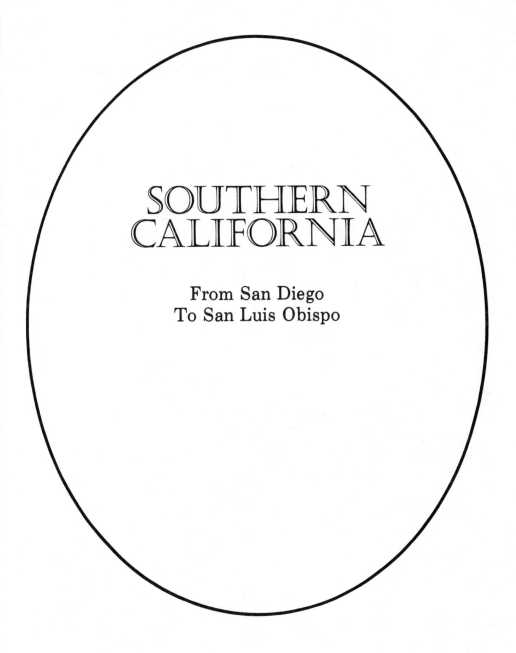

SOUTHERN CALIFORNIA

From San Diego
To San Luis Obispo

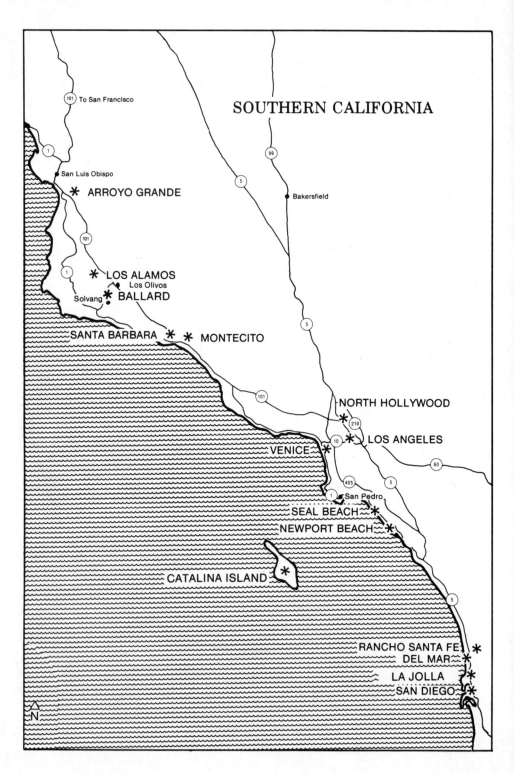

SOUTHERN CALIFORNIA

101 To San Francisco

1

San Luis Obispo

* ARROYO GRANDE

99

5

Bakersfield

101

1

* LOS ALAMOS
Los Olivos
Solvang * BALLARD

5

SANTA BARBARA * * MONTECITO

101

NORTH HOLLYWOOD
* 210
10 * LOS ANGELES
VENICE *

60

405
1 San Pedro
SEAL BEACH *
NEWPORT BEACH *

5

CATALINA ISLAND *

5

RANCHO SANTA FE *
DEL MAR *
LA JOLLA *
SAN DIEGO *

N

The Birthplace of California

SAN DIEGO

In 1542 the Spanish explorer Juan Rodriguez Cabrillo sailed into San Diego Bay. The first white man to set foot on California soil, he claimed the area for Spain, which proceeded to ignore its new territory for over two centuries. The Spanish were looking for gold and, ironically, could see no potential in this wilderness inhabited only by poor Indians, a wilderness that one day would provide the biggest gold strike in history. Finally, in 1769 Father Junípero Serra led a group of Franciscan padres to California, founding the state's first mission at San Diego. These priests became the state's first innkeepers, building a string of twenty-one missions up the coast, spaced a day's journey apart so that travelers could find food and lodging each night.

Today San Diego is the third-largest and one of the fastest-growing cities in the state. Besides being a major commercial and educational center (nine institutions of higher learning are located here), the city and its adjacent communities are a year-round vacation land. Water sports—from swimming off the sun-drenched beaches to deep-sea fishing off the coast—are popular diversions. San Diego also boasts one of the finest zoos in the country and Sea World, the largest oceanarium in the world, plus countless sightseeing opportunities. These include Old Town, the original Spanish settlement with many of the old adobes intact, and the Mission San Diego de Alcala. A short drive whisks you across the border to old Mexico.

Amid Eight Acres of Victoriana

HERITAGE PARK BED & BREAKFAST INN
Old Town, San Diego

On a hillside above historic Old Town, a meticulously landscaped eight-acre park—complete with cobblestone walkways and nineteenth-century streetlights—preserves some of San Diego's finest examples of Victorian architecture. Heritage Park is owned by the County of San Diego, which moved eight landmark houses here from other parts of the city, restored their exteriors and leased them for commercial ventures ranging from gift shops to law offices. Lori Chandler, an avid antiques collector and former teacher, converted one of the buildings, a splendid 1889 Queen Anne, into a bed and breakfast inn.

Before opening her inn in 1985, Lori spent some fifteen years researching the B&Bs of America. She chose an authentic approach to the decorating, leaving the lacquered redwood moldings in the high-ceilinged rooms, adorning the walls with William Morris papers, and filling the house with turn-of-the-century antiques and bric-a-brac. The furnishings are hard to describe, however, because what you see today may be gone tomorrow: the Victoriana is all for sale. Three bedrooms have the original tile fireplaces (now filled with plants), but Lori hopes to convert these to gas-burning hearths. And a turret room commands a view of downtown San Diego.

Breakfast is substantial at Heritage Park B&B—juices, fruit, freshly baked breads and a hot egg dish. It's either brought to your room on an antique tray or served outside on the wide veranda. For other meals you can stroll down the hill to Old Town or drive a few miles to San Diego's numerous fine restaurants. Or, with advance notice, the innkeeper will arrange for a country-style-barbecue supper or a five-course dinner to be served in your room at a candlelit table for two. And if you're still in the mood to stay home, Heritage Park provides another unusual amenity: every night a vintage film is shown on the VCR, which is the only modern device in the inn's old-fashioned parlor.

HERITAGE PARK BED & BREAKFAST INN, 2470 Heritage Park Row, San Diego, California 92110. Telephone: (619) 295-7088. Accommodations: nine rooms with double and queen-size beds; three rooms have private baths, six share three baths, stall shower or tub/shower; one room fully equipped for the handicapped; no telephones; no television. Rates: moderate to expensive, breakfast included. Children over 14 welcome. No pets. No smoking. Cards: MC, VISA. Open all year.

Getting There: From Highway 5, just north of downtown San Diego, take Old Town exit to San Diego Avenue. Turn left, then turn right on Harney, which leads into Heritage Park.

Heritage Park Bed & Breakfast Inn

BRITT HOUSE
San Diego

It seems fitting that the city where California's string of missions started should give birth to southern California's first bed and breakfast inn. In 1979—several years after the B&B craze hit the northern part of the state—designer Robert Hostick and home economics teacher Daun Martin opened the inn in a circa-1887 Queen Anne Victorian. The three-story house with its circular tower and gabled roof was built by attorney Eugene Britt; later, it was owned by newspaper publisher E. W. Scripps.

The most dramatic feature of the Britt House is a monumental entrance hall with intricate paneled wainscoting and a stairway of oak. Three stained-glass windows rise from floor to ceiling, and a filigree of spoolwork arches over the entrance to the parlor, which contains a baby grand piano.

Robert Hostick designed the interiors, opting for country charm rather than authenticity. Each room is papered in a different pattern, but color themes of blue, burgundy, rust and eggplant appear in many variations. In the ten bedrooms, periods of furnishings are mixed with considerable grace. Marble-topped Eastlake dressers and old platform rockers mingle with wicker and rattan and comfortable queen-size beds with quilted spreads. Gilt-framed "family portraits" adorn the dressers, and Hostick's own bright contemporary graphics hang on the walls.

Brightly colored rag dolls and stuffed animals recline around the bedrooms, and all have names. Harry the Hen inhabits the Music Room off the lower hall, and in another room, Elizabeth, a flamboyant ostrich, roosts on a velvet-canopied bed. Bouquets of silk and fresh flowers, bowls of fruit and homemade cookies are placed in all the rooms. Two rooms have private balconies. A garden cottage has a kitchenette and private bath. Four community baths offer guests some intriguing choices of bathing. One has two "his and her" claw-legged tubs, equipped with bubble bath. Another has a sauna.

Daun obviously has gone "the extra mile" in every detail of the Britt House, breakfast included. She or her assistant bakes individual loaves of a different yeast bread every day—nine-grain, orange, and carrot are a few—to serve on the bedroom trays, along with fresh-squeezed orange juice, shirred eggs and Viennese-roast coffee. A complimentary afternoon tea is also served, consisting of tea and a large variety of sweets and savories. And to help you with dinner plans, menus have been collected from the many fine restaurants in the area. The Britt House is only two blocks from the famed Balboa Park and San Diego Zoo, and it's only a ten-minute walk to the beach and the harbor.

BRITT HOUSE, 406 Maple Street, San Diego, California 92103. Telephone: (714) 234-2926. Accommodations: ten rooms with twin or queen-size beds; one room with private bath, others share four baths with tub or shower, one with wheelchair access; no telephones; no television. Rates: moderate to expensive, breakfast included. No children under 12, except in cottage. No pets. No smoking. Cards: AE, MC, VISA. Open all year.

Getting There: From Los Angeles take Highway 405 or Highway 5 south to San Diego's Washington Street exit, proceed east to Fourth Street, turn right on Fourth to Maple.

For Which the Bells Toll
THE BED & BREAKFAST INN AT LA JOLLA
La Jolla

A few miles north of San Diego, a hilly peninsula forested with Torrey pines juts into the Pacific. On its northern slopes, extending down to the beaches, lies the affluent community of La Jolla, with its showplace homes, fine shops and restaurants. Now, one of the older residences—built in 1913 in a cubist-southwestern style with surprisingly simple lines for that era—is the site of an exquisite B&B.

The house, where John Philip Sousa lived in the 1920s, has been elegantly refurbished by Betty Albee, former manager at The Bed & Breakfast Inn of San Francisco. The sixteen bedrooms are decorated in a variety of styles, ranging from a Laura Ashley country look with white wicker furniture to a more traditional mode with wing chairs and canopied beds. Throughout, Dhurrie rugs are scattered over polished pine floors. Bowls of fresh fruit and flowers are placed in the rooms, and heaps of pillows topped with a fortune cookie grace the beds. Three guest rooms have wood-burning fireplaces, and several have partial or full views of the ocean.

A sunny second-floor common room, stocked with lots of books and a television set, opens onto a big deck. Downstairs a pretty formal dining room looks out to a brick patio and a lawn surrounded by trees and gardens. You may choose to have your breakfast of juice, rolls and coffee downstairs or on the upper deck—or brought to your room.

From The Bed & Breakfast Inn it's an easy walk to La Jolla's shops and restaurants. The municipal tennis courts are across the street. And next door is St. James Church, where, every fifteen minutes during the day, the bells toll for guests at the inn.

THE BED & BREAKFAST INN AT LA JOLLA, 7753 Draper Avenue, La Jolla, California 92037. Telephone: (619) 456-2066. Accommodations: sixteen rooms with twin or queen-size beds; all but one have private baths with stall shower or tub/shower; one room with wheelchair access; telephones on request; no television. Rates: moderate to very expensive, breakfast included. Children over 12 welcome. No pets. Cards: MC, VISA. Open all year.

Getting There: From Highway 5, north of San Diego, take La Jolla Village Drive exit and turn right on Torrey Pines Road. Proceed for about five miles to Prospect, turn right and, when in town, turn left on Draper. Off-street parking available behind the inn.

Lovely Inn with a Shady Past

ROCK HAUS

Del Mar

Henry W. Keller was president of the South Coast Land Company which developed the beautiful beach resort of Del Mar just north of San Diego at the turn of the century. In 1910 he built a large summer home for his family on a hill overlooking the village and the Pacific. Constructed of stone and wood and surrounded by Torrey pines, the house is an elaborate version of the craftsman style so popular in southern California during this period. After auspicious beginnings— Sunday mass was conducted in the dining room and the big-name bands that came to the old Del Mar Hotel had jam sessions here—the hillside mansion became a private club in the 1920s and, for the next five decades, hosted almost every illicit activity imaginable. Old-timers remember frequent police busts for gambling and illegal alcohol, and they surmise that ladies of questionable morals frequented the establishment. In the 1950s new owners named the place Rock House Hotel and ran a boardinghouse that later, in the 1960s, turned into a hippie pad, rife with the smell of marijuana. It was also used as a safe house for smuggling Mexicans into California.

Then, in 1982, lawyer Tom Hauser and his wife, Carol, bought the old Rock House. After extensive renovation they turned it into an inn, renaming it Rock Haus. They laughingly point to a tombstone-like rock in front of the house. "We buried the hotel's sign there," Tom says, "and with it the saga of the Rock House Hotel." This is indeed a new era for the handsome building, which sits on an acre of groomed lawn and gardens. Carol has decorated the ten bedrooms to look like the rooms in a 1910 summer home should with lots of wicker and rattan, flowery comforters, mounds of ruffled pillows, little antique writing tables and some beds with canopies. Most of the upstairs rooms have fabulous ocean views, while four downstairs rooms, one with a fireplace, have private entrances.

Probably the most interesting guest room is the Whale Watch Room, a good place to bone up on the migration of the great gray whales that can be spotted all along the California coast during the winter months. These giant mammals leave their home in the Arctic and make a ten-thousand-mile round trip to have their babies in the warm lagoons off Baja California. The Hausers have placed *Moby Dick* and other works on whaleology in the room along with an 1861 chart of the whale migration and a replica of an old whalers' lodging sign, a reminder that San Diego was once a major whaling port. There's also a reminder of the inn's shady past: a paneled and mirrored headboard that once served as a false front for the area where the gambling tables were hidden off the living room.

Today this living room, with its beamed ceiling, stone fireplace and Oriental rugs on the hardwood floors, is the scene of more wholesome amenities: a player piano, backgammon set, and comfortable couches and chairs where you might want to curl up with a book from the Hausers' large library. Beverages are served here in the evening. A sun porch with a clear view of the Pacific is the setting for a light breakfast of fresh fruit, juice, and muffins or coffeecake.

The beach and the village shops are the chief attractions of Del Mar, except in the summer months, when the racetrack, built by Bing Crosby and Bob Hope in 1937, brings some fifty thousand horse-race fans to town. The many diversions of San Diego are only a short distance away. But Rock Haus is such a lovely inn, you might just want to while away your day there.

ROCK HAUS, 410 Fifteenth Street, Del Mar, California 92014. Telephone: (619) 481-3764. Accommodations: ten rooms with twin, queen- and king-size beds; six upstairs rooms share three baths with stall shower or tub; four downstairs rooms with private baths, stall shower; no telephones; no television. Rates: moderate to expensive, Continental breakfast included. No children. No pets. No smoking. Cards: MC, VISA. Open all year.

Getting There: From San Diego take Del Mar Heights exit off the San Diego Freeway and head west to Camino Del Mar, turn right to Fifteenth Street and turn right again. From Los Angeles take Via de la Valle exit off the San Diego Freeway and head southwest along Jimmy Durante Boulevard to the village of Del Mar, turn left on Fifteenth Street. Courtesy pickup at the Amtrak station in Del Mar.

Rock Haus

Twenty Acres of Gardens and Eucalyptus Trees

THE INN AT RANCHO SANTA FE

Rancho Santa Fe

The very exclusive community of Rancho Santa Fe consists of elegant tile-roofed houses set among dense eucalyptus groves in the hills inland from Del Mar beach. The hub of the area is a tiny village containing exquisite shops and the Inn. A century ago, however, this place was just a barren stretch of land that had been granted by the Mexican government to Juan Maria Osuna, one-time mayor of the Pueblo de San Diego. Then, in 1906, the Santa Fe Railroad purchased the land from Osuna's heirs, for the purpose of raising Australian eucalyptus for railroad ties—one of the most colossal agricultural follies in California history. Over three million seedlings were planted before Santa Fe officials realized that the gnarled eucalyptus wood was totally unsuitable for ties.

They recouped their investment by planting the remaining acres with citrus and by selling off the eucalyptus forests for home sites. A lovely Spanish-style adobe building was constructed to house prospective purchasers. This building—along with clusters of cottages scattered among twenty acres of woods, lawns, ivy-bedded walkways and gardens rife with bougainvillea, roses, magnolias and palms—is now the Inn.

The Royce family has owned the Inn since 1958 and Daniel Royce now manages it in a very personal fashion. In the living room, massive beams support a wooden ceiling that pitches some eighteen feet above the richly carpeted floor. Comfortable couches surround a fireplace, and Royce family antiques, including a large collection of old sailing-ship models, adorn the walls and tables. Four dining areas offer choices ranging from an alfresco terrace to a cozy book-lined library, and on balmy summer weekend nights there is dancing under the stars.

A wide range of accommodations here fits almost any budget. Most rooms in the main bulding have private lanais and are simply furnished with white wicker. Many of the cottage rooms have living rooms with fireplaces and some have kitchenettes; all have private patios, terraces or decks. These units were also designed with flexibility in mind so that rooms can be opened to each other to accommodate groups or families of various sizes.

Rancho Santa Fe has all the amenities of a fine resort hotel: Three tennis courts, a swimming pool and a croquet court are located on the grounds. Guest privileges are available at two private eighteen-hole golf courses nearby. And if you seek the beach, the Inn maintains a

The Inn at Rancho Santa Fe

seaside cottage with dressing rooms and showers at Del Mar, which is only a few minutes away.

THE INN AT RANCHO SANTA FE, Box 869, Rancho Santa Fe, California 92067. Telephone: (619) 756-1131. Accommodations: seventy-five rooms, most with twin beds and some with king-size beds; private baths with stall shower or tub/shower; telephones; television. Rates: moderate to very expensive, no meals included. Dining rooms open for breakfast, lunch and dinner; full bar service; room service available during dining room hours. Children welcome. One dog allowed in certain rooms at extra charge. Cards: AE, CB, DC, MC, VISA. Facilities for weddings and conferences. Open all year.

Getting There: From the San Diego Freeway take the Lomas Santa Fe Drive or the Via de la Valle exit and head east. Both roads lead to the Inn. For a nominal charge and with advance notice the Inn will pick up guests at the Amtrak station in Del Mar or at Lindbergh Field in San Diego.

A Bit of Barbary Coast on the Beach
DORYMAN'S INN
Newport Beach

The resort towns of Newport Beach and Balboa are built on a finger of land that juts from the coast to shelter a colorful harbor dotted with tiny islands and hundreds of pleasure boats—one of the major yachting centers on the California coast. On the ocean side of this peninsula, the Newport pier thrusts into the Pacific. In 1978 real estate developer Rick Lawrence acquired an old rooming house facing the pier and, after five years of renovation to the tune of two million dollars, opened a classy little inn. Doryman's looks for all the world like a Barbary Coast bordello, but one patronized by bankers and silver barons rather than boat handlers.

Two restaurants occupy the downstairs; inn guests enter through a private side door and are whisked by elevator to the second floor. Here, in the hallway, skylights are hung with plants, and shiny brass wall scounces adorn the oak wainscoting, which is polished to a mirrorlike finish. Each of the ten rooms has a gas-burning fireplace, controlled by the flick of a wall switch, with antique mantels imported from Europe. Bathrooms are outfitted with skylights and sunken tubs faced with Carrara marble, some with Jacuzzi spouts. The rooms are papered with reproductions of 1880 patterns, some with hand-stenciled friezes around the top. Matching floral drapes and quilted bedspreads, lace curtains, down comforters and pillows trimmed with eyelet ruffles add to the romantic aura. Furnishings are mostly European antiques: carved headboards, canopied four-posters, armoires, needlepoint chairs, rockers and gilt-edged mirrors abound. Five of the rooms have unobstructed views of the Pacific and several have french doors opening to a tiled balcony. A little sitting room also opens to this balcony. Guests may have their breakfast served here—a tray of orange juice, fresh fruit, soft-boiled eggs, and such treats as pumpkin or banana breads. But most prefer the luxury and privacy of breakfast in bed.

DORYMAN'S INN, 2102 West Ocean Front, Newport Beach, California 92663. Telephone: (714) 675-7300. Accommodations: ten rooms with queen- or king-size beds; private baths with tub/shower; telephones; color television. Rates: very expensive, breakfast included. No children under 16. No pets. Cards: AE, CB, DC, MC, VISA. Open all year except Halloween Eve.

Getting There: From the San Diego Freeway take the Harbor Boulevard or Costa Mesa Boulevard exit west to Newport Beach. After crossing Highway 1 continue on Newport Boulevard to Thirty-second Street, turn left on Balboa Boulevard and turn right at the sign to Newport Pier.

Old World Aura in a Flower-Filled Setting
THE SEAL BEACH INN & GARDENS
Seal Beach

During the 1920s Seal Beach was a popular playground for the wealthy residents of Hollywood and Pasadena. It was the last stop on an electric railway that later extended to Newport Beach, and during the town's heyday, gambling palaces, wooden bathhouses and small hotels abounded. The only hotel remaining from that era is the Seal Beach Inn, which Jack and Marjorie Bettenhausen have transformed into a charming Mediterranean-style hostelry. The rooms surround a brick-paved courtyard ablaze with roses, geraniums, jasmine, camellias, hibiscus and oleander. Fountains, statues and benches from France are scattered around, along with ornate old street lamps from Long Beach. On the second-floor veranda, filigreed white ironwork is entwined with flowering vines.

Ever since they purchased the place in 1977, the Bettenhausens have never stopped improving it—a true labor of love. They have shipped back truckloads of antiques and objets d'art from their frequent travels throughout the United States and Europe. The result is a potpourri of furnishings ranging from Early Americana to Renoir prints, from Victoriana to art nouveau. Hollywood also gets into the act: a four-poster headboard from John Barrymore's bed occupies one room, and a stained-glass door from Universal Studios opens to a bridal suite bedecked with lace and rose-colored satin.

The rooms range from tiny (about ten by twelve feet) to suites that have sitting areas and completely equipped kitchen bars. A penthouse suite has a flower-filled private deck, a large living room, a full kitchen with a breakfast nook, and two old-fashioned sleeping porches.

"The look of an inn is important," Marjorie says, "but loving people and being hospitable are even more important." And she does these things very well. Plenty of reading material is found in the downstairs library (as well as in the rooms), along with chess sets, Scrabble boards and puzzles to enjoy by the fire. In the adjoining tea room, an elaborate breakfast buffet is served—fresh fruit, house-made jams and jellies, the inn's own granola, boiled eggs and a variety of pastries and breads. Both common rooms open to a patio with another Hollywood touch—a kidney-shaped swimming pool.

Marjorie's hospitality extends to helping her guests enjoy Seal Beach. The ocean is only a block from the inn; amenities there include a pier, boat excursions, fishing and a windsurfing school. The inn will even pack a picnic for your day's excursion. The Long Beach Marina and its Seaport Village are only five blocks away. And there are shops, boutiques and eighteen restaurants in the area.

SEAL BEACH INN, 212 Fifth Street, Seal Beach, California 90740. Telephone: (213) 493-2416. Accommodations: twenty-three rooms with twin, double, queen- and king-size beds; private baths with stall shower or tub/shower; no telephones; color televisions. Rates: inexpensive to expensive, breakfast included. Children welcome. No pets. No smoking. Cards: AE, MC, VISA. Open all year.

Getting There: From Los Angeles take Highway 605 south to the San Diego Freeway south; take Seal Beach Boulevard exit and turn left to Highway 1; turn right and head north; turn left on Fifth Street.

THE INN ON MT. ADA
Santa Catalina Island

So you want to escape to a tropical isle for a romantic holiday in a palatial mountaintop hideaway. Consider The Inn on Mt. Ada on Catalina Island, just twenty-two miles off the California coast. The history of this lovely isle in some respects mirrors the saga of the Golden State. Friendly Indians inhabited Catalina when Juan Rodriguez Cabrillo discovered it in 1542. Later, the abundance of sea otters around the island lured American and Russian fur traders, and the secluded coves attracted smugglers of illegal Chinese immigrants and illicit cargoes. Catalina was even the site of a mining boom in the 1860s.

Since 1848, the island has been privately owned, but it was not really developed until 1919, when industrialist William Wrigley, Jr. (of chewing gum and Chicago Cubs fame) acquired Catalina. On the highest point above Avalon Bay, he built a spectacular Georgian colonial mansion as a summer home and played host to the rich and famous of the 1920s, including the Prince of Wales, who later became Edward VIII. In the summer of 1923, Wrigley painted the house white in honor of the impending visit of President Harding, who died in San Francisco en route to the island. Harding's successor Calvin Coolidge, however, did use the mansion on Mt. Ada as a summer retreat.

In 1978 the Santa Catalina Land Company gave the Wrigley mansion to the University of Southern California, which operated it as a conference center for a while. Then, in 1985, USC leased the building to a group of local residents for use as an inn.

The Inn on Mt. Ada, now elegantly restored, furnished with exquisite antiques and repainted its original gray, is flanked by broad decks and terraces that afford awe-inspiring views of the surrounding mountains, the town and port of Avalon far below and, on clear days, the California coast across the channel. The spacious rooms on the first floor include a seventy-foot-long formal drawing room, which boasts a fireplace, grand piano and french doors leading out to a terrace; a more casually furnished den, well stocked with games and complimentary soft drinks; a cozy study, and a plant-filled sun room equipped with telescope for admiring the view of the town. There's also a lovely dining room, where breakfast is served on small tables colorfully set with California pottery and flowered china. A typical menu includes orange juice, blueberries with cream, a mushroom-onion-cheese omelet and English muffins. In a pantry off the kitchen, freshly baked cookies, fruit and an assortment of coffees and teas are set out night and day.

The six guest rooms on the second floor offer a range of splendor (and price)—from Wrigley's former quarters (a grand suite with a large living room, fireplace and private terrace) to a tiny sun room surrounded by windows. In between, there's Ada Wrigley's room, which has a fireplace and a small sitting room with a chaise, and the corner guest room once occupied by Coolidge, which has a fireplace too. All the rooms have incredible views—even the baths.

Two of the inn's leaseholders, Susie Griffin and Marlene McAdam, serve as innkeepers and are happy to give advice on the island's activities. These include tennis, golf, horseback riding and, of course, swimming, snorkeling, and scuba diving in the sapphire-clear waters of the bay. Curio shops and mobs of tourists have somewhat tarnished the picturesque town of Avalon, but most of the island—some forty-two-thousand acres—is now an untouched wilderness preserve that nature lovers can explore. Though Avalon has a number of restaurants, none share Mt. Ada's world-class status. But if you book the entire inn, Susie or Marlene will arrange for catered dinners befitting the elegance of this hilltop showplace.

THE INN ON MT. ADA, #1 Wrigley Road (P.O. Box 2560), Avalon, California 90704. Telephone: (213) 510-2030. Accommodations: six rooms with double or queen-size beds; private baths with stall shower or tub/shower; no telephones; television on request. Rates: very expensive, breakfast included. Children over 14 welcome. No pets. No smoking. Cards: AE, MC, VISA. Facilities for weddings and conferences. Open all year.

Getting There: Catalina may be reached from the mainland by seventeen-minute helicopter and thirty-minute airplane flights, but the ideal approach is by boat. The fastest boat passage is a ninety-minute crossing from San Pedro on comfortable 149-passenger vessels operated by Catalina Express, P.O. Box 1391, San Pedro, California 90733; telephone (213) 519-1212. Visitors are not permitted to take automobiles to Catalina, but car and bike rentals are available there. The Inn on Mt. Ada has arranged complimentary taxi service for its guests to and from the town of Avalon.

The Inn on Mt. Ada

THE VENICE BEACH HOUSE
Venice

At the turn of the century, when Abbot Kinney bought a stretch of coastal marshland just outside Los Angeles with the dream of re-creating Venice, skeptical Californians nicknamed this beach area Abbot's folly. Kinney constructed canals, bathhouses, elegant hotels, boardwalks, long piers and an amusement park and encouraged the staging of art exhibitions and other cultural events. By 1906, when Sarah Bernhardt played to a full house for three nights in Venice, Angelenos had stopped scoffing at Kinney and were flocking to his new resort. In 1911, one of these converts, Warren Wilson, wealthy publisher of the *Los Angeles Daily Journal,* built a spacious house in the California craftsman style a half-block from the beach. Two of Wilson's daughters married Kinney's sons.

The Wilson family owned the property for some forty years, but meanwhile, Venice was heading downhill. Oil was being drilled offshore, many of the canals were filled in, the old houses were cut up or torn down to make room for cheap apartments, the amusement park was demolished, and in the 1960s hippies virtually took over the town. Kinney's dream had indeed become a folly.

But today the pendulum is swinging in Venice's favor. The Marina del Rey, a fancy apartment complex, was built next door; the oil derricks are gone, leaving the beach clean and fine for swimming; and the seaside properties are now predominately upper-middle-class residences.

Among those who rediscovered Venice was Philip Boesch, a young attorney from New England. He bought the old Warren house, which had been converted to apartments, simply because he loved it and wanted to restore it. Now the handsome gray shingled house is surrounded by manicured lawns and gardens. In the wood-beamed living room, the soft gray, rose and mauve hues of an enormous Oriental rug orchestrate the color scheme for much of the house. Comfortable chairs and a sofa, upholstered in shades of mauve, are set around the large brick fireplace, and an adjoining sun room offers an ocean view and a breakfast buffet. Breakfast can be eaten at little tables with flowered skirts or out on the wide veranda that fronts the house.

Bedroom walls are covered with padded fabrics that match the bedspreads—an ingenious soundproofing device. In the first-floor bedroom, which overlooks the garden, the motif is mauve-and-rose hydrangeas printed on silk. Upstairs, the most expensive room—which has a fireplace, ocean view and private sun porch—is tailored in gray wool tweed with accents of mauve. In another, the walls and a canopied bed are dressed in frilly Laura Ashley prints; a contrasting, very masculine room is resplendent with wool tartan plaids. Even the bathrooms are romantic here: one has double shower spigots, one is outfitted with a Jacuzzi tub for two, and another contains two old-fashioned tubs with gilded claws.

Whether you come to Los Angeles to play or to work, Venice is a convenient location. The inn provides bicycles for pedaling along the beach trail, which extends from Santa Monica to Long Beach. There's night life aplenty in the bustling bars and bistros of neighboring Marina del Rey. Beverly Hills and Century City are about fifteen minutes away, and downtown Los Angeles is a half-hour drive.

THE VENICE BEACH HOUSE, 15 Thirtieth Avenue, Venice, California 90291. Telephone: (213) 823-1966. Accommodations: nine rooms with twin, two doubles, queen- or king-size beds; some private and some shared baths, tub/shower; telephones and cable television available on request. Rates: inexpensive to expensive. No children under 10. No pets. No smoking. Cards: AE, MC, VISA. Open all year.

Getting There: From the San Diego Freeway, take the Washington Boulevard exit south of Santa Monica and head west. Where Washington forks, follow Washington Street to the beach and turn right on Speedway, the last street before the boardwalk. At Twenty-Ninth Avenue, turn right into the inn's parking area.

SALISBURY HOUSE

Los Angeles

Early in this century—before the movie makers discovered California—Los Angeles was a sleepy town compared with boisterous San Francisco. Its affluent citizens lived several miles west of downtown, separated from the Pacific by ranches and citrus groves, in unpretentious houses predominately of the woodsy craftsman style. This area, now Arlington Heights, began to decline after World War I and was further damaged when the Santa Monica Freeway cut through the middle of it. But in recent years, especially with the redevelopment of downtown and the construction of the Convention Center, Angelenos have begun to appreciate the heritage evoked by these fine old houses, and the district is gradually being renovated. Here, on a quiet residential street, Kathleen Salisbury opened Los Angeles' first B&B.

The two-story Salisbury House, which is topped with a gabled attic, was built in 1909. The downstairs is notable for the rich woodwork of dark fir, leaded glass windows and beamed ceilings so typical of the craftsman style. Kathleen, an interior designer, has created an old-fashioned country look with flowered wallpaper in the Laura Ashley mode; collections of Delft china, displayed on plate racks; and antique dolls set about here and there. The living room is homey, with overstuffed couches covered with floral prints, Oriental

rugs, lace café curtains and a wood-burning fireplace. The upstairs bedrooms are also abloom with floral-print wallpaper, curtains, comforters and ruffled pillows. Furnishings are European and American wood and wicker antiques. One room has an adjoining sun room with a trundle bed; it's a sitting room by day and a twin-bedded sleeping room by night. The cozy attic, with a quadruple-gabled roof and pine paneling, also has a sitting area and a bathrub in the room.

Many of the Salisbury guests are business travelers, and Kathleen does not send them off to a day's work hungry. Breakfast, served in the formal dining room, is a hearty meal: orange juice, a fruit dish such as apple dumpling or peach-and-raspberry melba, homemade muffins or fruit breads, and a main course that varies from quiche to frittata to sherried crab in a pastry shell. Long-staying guests appreciate this variety as well as the proximity of downtown, which is only minutes away.

SALISBURY HOUSE, 2273 West Twentieth Street, Los Angeles, California 90018. Telephone: (213) 737-7817. Accommodations: five rooms with double, queen- or king-size beds; three private baths and one shared bath with tub, tub/shower or stall shower; no telephones; television sets available on request. Rates: inexpensive to moderate, breakfast included. Children over 10 welcome. No pets. Cards: AE, MC, VISA. Facilities for small conferences. Open all year.

Getting There: The inn is off the Santa Monica Freeway, which connects downtown Los Angeles with the San Diego Freeway. Take the Western Avenue exit one block to the north and turn left on Twentieth.

Artistry in a Mediterranean Villa
LA MAIDA HOUSE
North Hollywood

This Mediterranean-style villa, surrounded by tiled patios, lush lawns and gardens, would be a sensational setting for anyone's inn. But the creativity and boundless energy of owner Megan Timothy make a stay at La Maida an exquisite experience that would be difficult to match anywhere. Megan's artistry is reflected in every aspect of the inn, from the ninety-seven stained-glass windows she has designed and executed throughout the house to the sculptured pat of butter on the breakfast plate.

Antonio La Maida, an expatriate Italian, built the villa in 1926 on a large estate that has since been subdivided. The white stucco walls,

23

red-tiled roof, arched windows, tiled patios and fountains and lavish use of fine woods and wrought iron are typical of the mansions built in Hollywood during the 1920s. The high-ceilinged living room, down a few steps from the entry hall, boasts polished oak floors, a Carrara marble fireplace and an 1881 grand piano that once belonged to bandleader Horace Heidt. An adjoining den is almost completely filled with tiers of wall-to-wall studio couches of various heights, upholstered in a rust-colored fabric and massed with pillows; one side of this unique room opens to an enclosed tiled patio, where light filters through a stained-glass ceiling onto scores of tropical plants. Glass doors open from here to the lovely gardens where fountains tinkle under the shade of a large magnolia tree, flowers bloom year round, and two black swans glide around a pond.

Four bedrooms are located upstairs, each stunningly decorated in a different style. In the largest, a canopied king-size bed is framed with rough-hewn wood, and a rattan chaise, table and chairs provide a comfortable spot for the tray of pre-breakfast tea and coffee that is brought each morning. Another room features turn-of-the-century furnishings; another is done in white wicker; and the fourth opens to a balcony. All the rooms are appointed with plants, cut flowers from La Maida's gardens, complimentary toiletries, terrycloth robes and knee robes crocheted by Megan's mother, Helen, who helps manage the inn. Across the street from the main villa are two smaller houses that are also part of the inn. Several of these units are suites with fireplaces (one suite has a complete kitchen), and many of the rooms have private patios or gardens and/or Jacuzzi tubs.

Breakfast—or lunch or dinner by appointment—is served in one of three dining areas. If the group numbers four or less and the weather is fine, the setting might be a little second-floor balcony overlooking the garden. For eight, Megan sets the glass-topped table in a small dining room next to the enclosed downstairs patio; if guests wish to host dinners here, the den is used for the service of aperitifs. Finally, a large formal dining room, lit by candles and a crystal chandelier, provides seating for thirty-two at round tables.

Megan's culinary talents are remarkable; she runs a catering business, and her recipes have appeared in many national magazines. There are no set menus at La Maida House ("That would be boring") and everything—even the croissants and jams—is made from scratch and far from ordinary. The breakfast juice, for example, might be orange, flavored with a hint of cinnamon or blended with carrot juice; or a combination of apple and celery. Suppers are custom planned to the guest's wishes and they range from a simple soup and salad for two to

La Maida House

an elaborate four-course feast presented with artful garnishings on gold-rimmed Limoges china. With advance notice Megan will also put up picnic baskets complete with real plates—no paper or plastic here— for jaunts to the Hollywood Bowl, which is just a few minutes away.

La Maida House is also only minutes from Universal Studios and the NBC television studios, both of which conduct tours throughout each day. Hollywood, Beverly Hills and downtown Los Angeles are less than twenty minutes away.

LA MAIDA HOUSE, 11159 La Maida Street, North Hollywood, California 91601. Telephone: (818) 769-3857. Accommodations: ten rooms with twin, double, queen- and king-size beds; private baths with tub/shower or stall shower, some with Jacuzzis; direct-line telephones; television on request; air conditioned. Rates: moderate to expensive, Continental breakfast included; lunch and dinner served with advance notice at extra charge. No children under 16. No pets. No smoking. No credit cards. Facilities for weddings. Open all year.

Getting There: La Maida House is located near the intersection of the Hollywood and Ventura freeways. From the Hollywood Freeway (Highway 170), take the Magnolia exit, turn east to Tujunga Boulevard and turn right; then turn left on Camarillo Street and left on Bellflower to La Maida. From the west on the Ventura Freeway (Highway 101), take the Tujunga exit, turn right on Camarillo and proceed as above. From the east on the Ventura Freeway (Highway 134), take the Launkershim Boulevard exit north several blocks to La Maida and turn left.

A Romantic Retreat for Lovers Only
ROSEHOLM
Ventura/Ojai

Roseholm is for lovers only. This is not a place to bring your aunt or your kids or to stay by yourself. Everything is for two: the little skirted tables in the dining and living rooms, the Jacuzzi tubs in most of the guest rooms, the lace-covered queen-size beds. And every couple is treated like honeymooners. When you arrive in your room, you'll find a bottle of champagne, a basket of cheeses and a dozen red roses. In most rooms, there's a fireplace, too.

Roseholm delights all the senses. The pink stucco Mediterranean-style mansion, surrounded by gigantic oaks, looks like a storybook house. Classical music is piped inside and out, water splashes from gargoyled fountains in the patio, and you can hear the soft cooing of doves. All of the rooms, perfumed with fresh roses, have views of the countryside, and most overlook an adjoining brook and meadow, where you'll often see flocks of geese, ducks or blue herons.

Every afternoon, promptly at four, high tea is served: a sumptuous repast of five to eight hors d'oeuvres—perhaps salmon mousse, Cognac-spiked chicken-liver pâté, asparagus rolled with prosciutto, Scotch eggs, date-nut bread with cream cheese, and fresh strawberries. Although excellent restaurants in Ojai are only ten minutes away, few Roseholm guests go out for dinner. If you would like to take some liquid refreshments back to your room, you can help yourself. And if you get hungry later in the evening, you'll find dessert set out on the buffet.

In the morning a full breakfast is served, with entrées such as eggs Benedict or Yorkshire pudding with Italian sausage. You can retire to your room if you like, but if all the romance is getting too heady, Roseholm offers other things to do. In the garden you'll find an unusual swim spa; steelhead abound in the creek; and bird-watchers estimate that at least five hundred kinds of winged creatures inhabit the meadow. Indoors, readers will delight in the library's wall-to-wall collection of books, and in the living room, a grand piano and an 1860s pump organ await the musically inclined.

Roseholm is very, very expensive. But owners Jan and Patti Harmonson say that some guests think it's a bargain, since you pay nothing extra for all the food and drink. You've paid for ultimate privacy, too: the Harmonsons permit no visitors on the premises when the inn is occupied by overnight guests.

ROSEHOLM, 51 Sulphur Mountain Road, Ventura, California 93001. Telephone: (805) 649-4014. Accommodations: nine rooms or suites with queen-size beds; private baths, most with Jacuzzi tubs; no telephones; no television. Rates: very expensive, all food and beverages included. No children. No pets. No smoking. Cards: AE, MC, VISA. Open all year.

Getting There: From Los Angeles or San Francisco, take Highway 101 to Ventura and head east towards Ojai on Highway 33. Just beyond Casitas Springs, turn right on Sulphur Mountain Road.

California's Own Riviera
SANTA BARBARA

In 1786 the Spanish padres founded their tenth mission at the base of the Santa Ynez Mountains, which rise from the bay at Santa Barbara. After the 1812 earthquake, the mission was rebuilt and became known as Queen of the Missions for the beauty of its Moorish-Spanish architecture and the affluence of the surrounding ranches, orchards, gardens and vineyards. The resort city of Santa Barbara still retains the aura of its Spanish heritage. Red-tile–roofed buildings and old adobes, many enclosing inner patios, grace the palm-lined streets. There are splendid beaches, sportfishing, and botanical and zoological gardens. Excellent restaurants abound. The Santa Barbara Museum of Art houses a number of international collections; other museums focus on local history and natural history. And a visit to the mission, one of the most beautiful and well preserved in the state, recalls the days when the padres were this city's only innkeepers.

Getting There: From San Francisco or Los Angeles, Highway 101 leads directly to Santa Barbara, which is also serviced by United Airlines and Amtrak.

Over Five Hundred Acres of Privacy
SAN YSIDRO RANCH
Montecito

Among the vast holdings of Mission Santa Barbara was San Ysidro, a citrus and cattle ranch high in the Santa Ynez Mountains, with views of the oak-studded hills sloping to the Pacific far below. After the missions were secularized, new owners built rustic stone and wooden cottages among the groves of orange trees, eucalyptuses and palms, and alongside a meandering creek. By 1893, San Ysidro had become a guest ranch. The old adobe, built by the Franciscans in 1825, still stands, and guests dine today in a stone building once used as a citrus packing house.

San Ysidro's first illustrious era was in the 1930s and 1940s, when Ronald Colman and state Senator Alvin Weingand jointly owned the ranch. The guest book from those years reads like a combination of *Burke's Peerage* and *Who's Who* in politics, literature and show

San Ysidro Ranch

business. Sir Winston Churchill wrote part of his memoirs in a house shaded by a large magnolia tree. William Somerset Maugham produced several short stories in a cottage banked by geraniums. John Galsworthy sought seclusion here to work on the *Forsyte Saga*. David Niven, Merle Oberon and Rex Harrison found life at the ranch a respite from the glitter of Hollywood. Laurence Olivier and Vivien Leigh were married in the gardens. And later, John F. Kennedy brought his bride to an ivy-covered stone cottage at San Ysidro for their honeymoon.

After Colman and Weingand, San Ysidro had a succession of owners. Through years of neglect, its facilities degenerated, along with its reputation. The ranch was in deplorable condition by 1976, when it was purchased by Jim Lavenson, former president of the Plaza Hotel in New York City, and his wife, Susie. The Lavensons launched a crash renovation program, painting the cottages inside and out and bringing the lush gardens back to life. Susie was, and still is, the chief decorator: she has charmingly furnished the rooms with priceless family antiques from their New York home; these relics are interspersed with refinished artifacts culled from thrift shops and the Salvation Army.

Within a year, the ranch was operating in a style equal to the Colman-Weingand days, but that wasn't enough for the Lavensons. They embarked on phase two of the rehabilitation: Two more cottages, containing five units, were built, featuring soaring ceilings, fireplaces and private decks (three with sunk-in/tiled Jacuzzi tubs). Then, one at a time, the Lavensons gutted the interiors of the older buildings, removing the low ceilings in some to expose the beamed pitch of the roof, adding modern baths with sinks set into old-fashioned sideboards or dressers, combining small rooms into larger ones, rebricking hearths or adding fireplaces, rebuilding sagging decks, and adding wet bars and Jacuzzis to many units.

Old-time San Ysidro visitors might be astounded at the comforts found within the cottages today, but otherwise they would feel right at home. Except for fresh paint, the buildings' exteriors remain the same. The lovely gardens are abloom with marigolds, daisies, roses and geraniums, and the orchards are spangled with oranges, which guests are free to pick. The stables shelter fine riding horses, and the mountains that rise behind the inn offer 550 acres of isolated hiking trails. In fact privacy is a very important part of the San Ysidro tradition: The cottages are so self-contained that, with room service provided, you never need emerge—and some guests never do.

On the other hand, those looking for action will find it on the inn's three tennis courts, around the large swimming pool or in the main hacienda, which contains a piano, game tables and a chess board. Here, coffee brews twenty-four hours a day, and in the evening an honor bar is set up: guests mix their own drinks and write their own chits. Across the way, the attractive dining room has been chalking up Holiday Awards for its meals, which range from hearty alfresco breakfasts to candlelit gourmet dinners. And for evening entertainment, there's an excellent pianist in the stone cellar below. Despite all the amenities, San Ysidro is more casual and relaxed than most fancy resort hotels; Jim Lavenson's boots and blue jeans set the tone.

SAN YSIDRO RANCH, 900 San Ysidro Lane, Montecito, California 93108. Telephone: (805) 969-5046. Accommodations: twin, queen- or king-size beds; private baths with tub/shower; telephones; no television. Rates: very expensive, no meals included; extra charges for tennis and horseback riding. Open to the public for breakfast, lunch and dinner; full bar service. Children welcome. Extra charge for pets and for boarding horses. Cards: AE, MC, VISA. Facilities for conferences and weddings. Open all year.

Getting There: From Santa Barbara take Highway 101 south to Montecito; take San Ysidro Road east through Montecito Village to San Ysidro Lane.

A Facelifting for The Southland's Oldest Hotel

THE UPHAM
Santa Barbara

Over a century ago Amasa Lincoln, a transplanted Boston banker and distant cousin of Abraham Lincoln, decided that Santa Barbara needed a New England-style boardinghouse for homesick easterners. He hired the best architect in town to erect a two-story structure flanked by a columned veranda and topped with a cupola and widow's walk. In the early days the Chinese cook would send his assistant up here when the schooners landed to receive flag signals from a helper at the dock as to how many new guests would be at dinner that night. Over the years a series of owners added two other two-story buildings and four garden cottages to the Upham. In the past few decades the place has been a bit run-down; nevertheless, Santa Barbara natives and visitors alike regarded southern California's oldest continuously operated hotel with fondness and respect.

31

Then in 1982 Carl Johnson, a local developer who had just finished renovating the Hotel St. Helena, bought The Upham and hired Tom Brooks, one of the St. Helena's designers, to work his magic on the interior. The first-floor public rooms have been reconstructed to house a cheerful sun porch furnished with rattan, where wine is poured in the evening, and a large lobby with a fireplace surrounded by velvet-covered love seats. Along one side a row of tables, skirted with a flowered print, looks into the gardens. A Continental breakfast is served to hotel guests here, and Louie's restaurant alongside the veranda is open to the public for lunch and dinner.

In the guest rooms and cottages Brooks has mixed antiques—four-poster beds, old writing desks and armoires from England—with bold, sophisticated color schemes, quilted spreads of contemporary designs (often striped or geometric patterns) and white wide-louvered shutters. Earth colors—sand, brick and chocolate brown—contrast with the navy-blue carpeting found throughout. Some of the cottages have sitting rooms, fireplaces, private decks and Jacuzzi tubs. These units are reached by pathways through gardens abloom with pansies, roses, camelias and birds-of-paradise. The setting is countrylike, yet The Upham is only a block away from the smart shops and restaurants of State Street.

THE UPHAM, 1404 De la Vina Street, Santa Barbara, California 93101. Telephone: (805) 962-0058. Accommodations: fifty rooms with two double, queen- or king-size beds; private baths with tub or tub/shower; telephones; color television concealed in armoires. Rates: moderate to expensive, Continental breakfast included. Children welcome. No pets. Cards: MC, VISA. Open all year.

Getting There: From the north take Mission Street exit from Highway 101 and head east to De la Vina, proceed to Sala and turn left one-half block to the hotel's carriage entrance. From the south, exit from Highway 101 at State Street, turn right to Sala and turn left.

The Upham

The Enchantment of the Côte d'Azur
EL ENCANTO HOTEL
Santa Barbara

High in the hills above Santa Barbara's old mission, this gracious Mediterranean-style hotel offers breathtaking views of the city, the Pacific Ocean and the Channel Islands. The main building was built in 1915 to provide student-faculty housing for the University of California campus that was originally located across the way. Over the years bungalows and stucco villas were built in the surrounding ten aces of lush tropical gardens. El Encanto has been operated as a hotel since the mid-1930s, but Eric Friden, who bought it in 1977, has imparted the enchantment of an auberge on the French Riviera.

Window boxes filled with geraniums flank the canopied entryway. The public rooms are a visual symphony, orchestrated with many different fabrics in shades of forest green and mauve, natural woods and an abundance of plants. A spacious lounge is filled with chairs of wicker and rattan cushioned in a variety of patterns. Fireplaces and love seats upholstered in floral prints grace the cozy living room and adjoining library. And in the dining room, flowered wallpaper harmonizes with provincial-patterned chinaware, ceiling fans slowly revolve overhead, and large windows frame the dramatic view. Meals are also served outside under colorful umbrellas on two levels of terraces. The nouvelle cuisine is the work of a chef from Lyon.

El Encanto's gardens are planted with bougainvillea, hibiscus, banana trees, pines and palms. Bird-of-paradise and petunias border the brick walkways that lead to the guest cottages. All of the units have been extensively remodeled with modern tiled baths and new carpeting. Many have kitchens or wet bars and refrigerators, and the most lavish have fireplaces and private balconies or patios, some with tiled fountains. And to show that children are really welcome here, one suite now includes a nursery with a crib and an old-fashioned wicker high chair. In 1978 Friden constructed a two-story building of contemporary design that contains another twenty two-room units. These have corner fireplaces, wet bars, and balconies or patios, but the bedrooms are smaller than in the older buildings. Part of the enchantment of El Encanto is a turned-down bed at night and a small decanter of Armagnac placed beside the bed.

The hotel has a tennis court and a lovely swimming pool, but one of the greatest pleasures here is strolling the beautiful grounds, where swinging love seats are scattered about the lawns and an ancient grape

El Encanto Hotel

arbor encloses a lily-filled reflecting pool. Whether a guest at El Encanto or not, every visitor to Santa Barbara should at least come here for a drink at sunset. Looking down on the tile-roofed town and the sea beyond, you would truly think you were on the Côte d'Azur rather than the coast of California.

EL ENCANTO HOTEL AND GARDEN VILLAS, 1900 Lasuen Road, Santa Barbara, California, 93103. Telephone: (805) 687-5000. Accommodations: one hundred rooms with two double or king-size beds; private baths, with tub/shower; telephones; color television. Rates: expensive to very expensive, no meals included. Open to the public for breakfast, lunch, dinner and Sunday brunch; full bar service. Children welcome. No pets. Cards: AE, MC, VISA. Conference facilities. Open all year.

Getting There: From Highway 101, take Mission Street exit east; when road ends at Laguna, turn left at the Mission, then turn right on Los Olivos; where road forks, take right fork, Alameda Padre Serra; from here follow signs to El Encanto.

A Spanish Colonial Jewel

VILLA ROSA
Santa Barbara

Santa Barbara architecture immediately brings to mind white Spanish-style buildings embellished with ornate wooden balconies, wrought-iron grillwork, red tile roofs, arched windows and interior patios filled with fountains and tropical foliage. A classic of this style has now been turned into an inn and it's only half a block from the beach. Four Santa Barbarans—architect Mark Kirkhart, builder Robert Young and their wives—are responsible for the half-million-dollar renovation project that transformed this run-down, fifty-year-old apartment house into a jewel of a little hotel.

The exterior design was already there, but the inside was virtually rebuilt and strikingly decorated in a contemporary southwestern fashion. Desert hues of slate, sand and rosy terra-cotta are used throughout and the sturdy mission-style furniture was manufactured in Santa Fe. Couches and chairs are upholstered in handsome wool tweeds, beds are covered with woven spreads and rosy sheets, and Navajo blankets are hung on many of the walls. Some of the seventeen guest units are one- or two-story suites, several with fireplaces and kitchenettes. Other rooms have mullioned glass doors opening to private balconies—some with an ocean view—or to the large interior courtyard.

Here a swimming pool and spa are set among a melange of palm trees, banana groves and pots of colorful flowers. Also opening to the patio is the lovely living room with its high beamed ceiling and wood-burning fireplace faced with tile. Adjoining is a cozy lounge where a Continental breakfast is served and refreshments are offered in the evening. The Villa Rosa bids each guest good night by placing a long-stemmed red rose on the pillow of the turned-down bed.

VILLA ROSA, 15 Chapala Street, Santa Barbara, California 93101. Telephone: (805) 966-0851. Accommodations: seventeen rooms with queen- or king-size beds; private baths with tub/shower; telephones; no television. Rates: expensive to very expensive, Continental breakfast included. No children under 14. No pets. Cards: AE, MC, VISA. Open all year.

Getting There: Exit from Highway 101 at Chapala and head toward the beach.

Bed and Breakfast a Block from the Beach
THE OLD YACHT CLUB INN
Santa Barbara

The Old Yacht Club Inn was the first of Santa Barbara's B&Bs. The two-story bungalow was built in 1912, facing the beach, and for a while it served as temporary headquarters for the Santa Barbara Yacht Club, which had washed out to sea in a storm. Thus the name, though nothing else is nautical here. The house was moved a block inland from the beach in the 1920s and is now decorated with homey, country-style furnishings. The large living room-dining area has a fireplace and a bookcase stocked with a set of the Harvard Classics. Big windows look out onto a wide front porch, lawn and gardens. Innkeeper Nancy Donaldson loves to cook and puts a lot of effort into the breakfasts. She usually serves an omelet (perhaps zucchini or spinach) or french toast, in addition to home-baked breads, fruit and juice. She will also cook a five-course dinner on weekends for her guests.

The four upstairs bedrooms are decorated primarily in warm shades of rose and gold, with print spreads and matching draperies edging the lace-curtained windows. Fresh flowers are set on the tables. In the two front rooms, french doors open to a private balcony where you can hear the ocean, though it's obscured from view. A fifth bedroom with a sitting area and private bath is located downstairs.

In 1983 the Old Yacht Club's four owners acquired the house next door and each decorated one guest room there to reflect her own background, using family memorabilia. The Hitchcock House, as it is called, might be preferred by those looking for privacy: each bedroom has its own bath and outside entrance.

THE OLD YACHT CLUB INN, 431 Corona Del Mar, Santa Barbara, California 93103. Telephone: (805) 962-1277. Accommodations: five bedrooms within the inn with double, queen- or king-size beds; one with private bath, four rooms with sinks share two baths with tub/shower or stall shower; four rooms in Hitchcock House with queen- or king-size beds and private baths with tub/shower or shower; no telephones; no television. Rates: moderate to expensive, breakfast included, dinner (with advance notice) extra. Children over 14 welcome. No pets. No smoking. Cards: AE, MC, VISA. Open all year.

Getting There: Take Cabrillo Boulevard exit off Highway 101 toward the beach; just past the Sheraton Hotel, turn right on Corona Del Mar.

Proud of its Personal Services
THE GLENBOROUGH INN
Santa Barbara

A number of Santa Barbara's other B&Bs are located within a few blocks of each other in a residential area close to the downtown shops, restaurants and museums and an easy bike ride from the mission. Glenborough was the first of these inns to open. Innkeepers Jo Ann Bell and Pat Hardy have decorated the turn-of-the-century house in an old-fashioned style. The small, formal parlor has a velvet-upholstered settee pulled up to a Franklin stove. An old Victrola is stocked with records.

Most of the four upstairs bedrooms are furnished with antiques: brass or oak or four-poster beds, patchwork or velvet quilts, marble-topped chests, wickerware and curtains of old textiles, crochet, knitting

38

or lace. The *pièce de résistance,* though, is the new downstairs suite, all done up in art deco with a cast-iron stove in the parlor, a canopied bed and a private deck and garden. Glenborough also offers quarters across the street in a restored 1880s Victorian cottage with spacious gardens. Each unit here has a private entry, two have sitting rooms with fireplaces, and one has its own deck.

Jo Ann and Pat take pride in the small personal touches they provide: flowers, plants, and decanters of purified water in the rooms; beds turned down at night with a mint on the pillow; towels and soap changed twice daily. Breakfast is very special at Glenborough. Pat loves to cook and pampers her guests' palates as well as their health. Her meals are prepared without salt and with low-fat, low-cholesterol ingredients. Her menus vary: a favorite is "Santa Barbara Spanish"— huevos rancheros, flour tortillas sprinkled with cinnamon sugar, sliced grapefruit and fresh berries. In the main house, breakfast is delivered to your room (or the garden, if you like) on trays set with Haviland china and sterling silver. To guests in the cottage, breakfast is brought in a basket on colorful California pottery.

Behind the rear lawn of the main house is a Jacuzzi, completely fenced for privacy, which may also be used by guests staying in the cottage. They are also invited for beverages and homemade hors d'oeuvres in Glenborough's parlor each night.

THE GLENBOROUGH INN, 1327 Bath Street, Santa Barbara, California 93101. Telephone: (805) 966-0589. Accommodations: eight rooms with double or queen-size beds; two shared baths with tub/

39

shower in main house; other rooms have private baths; no telephones; no television. Rates: inexpensive to expensive, breakfast included. Children over 12 welcome. No pets. No smoking in main house. Cards: MC, VISA. Open all year.

Getting There: Take Carrillo exit off Highway 101 and head east to Bath; turn left.

Sun-Splashed Victorian with Ocean Views
THE PARSONAGE
Santa Barbara

In 1892, on a hillside above Santa Barbara, the Trinity Episcopal Church built a splendid Queen Anne residence to serve as a parsonage. The good reverend must have worshipped the sun along with his professed deity, because—unlike most Victorians—the house is splashed with light through a multitude of large windows of both clear and leaded glass. When interior designer Hilde Michelmore bought the place in 1981, it had been completely renovated into an inn, but her decorating talents and an impressive collection of Chinese rugs have made the sunny rooms truly sparkle.

Each room derives its theme and color scheme from its rug. In the living room, for example, a green-and-lilac floral motif is echoed in the upholstery of an oversized couch. On days when the sun is not pouring in from the corner windows, a fire burns in the hearth and also in the formal dining room with its large glassed-in bay. Here or on a spacious outside deck, Hilde serves a large breakfast that includes scrambled eggs, french toast or quiche, and nut or date breads.

Two of the upstairs guest rooms offer picturesque views of the city and ocean. One of these adjoins a private solarium with three walls of glass and an enormous bathroom. The bedrooms contain turn-of-the-century furnishings—armoires, draped or canopied beds, marble-topped pieces and, as downstairs, the handsome rugs.

THE PARSONAGE, 1600 Olive Street, Santa Barbara, California 93101. Telephone: (805) 962-9336. Accommodations: five rooms with twin, queen- or king-size beds; private baths with tub/shower or stall shower; no telephones; television in living room. Rates: moderate to expensive, breakfast included. Children over 14 welcome. No pets. Smoking discouraged. Cards: MC, VISA. Open all year.

The Parsonage

Getting There: From the north, take Mission Street exit from Highway 101 east to Laguna Street and turn right for one block; turn left on Olive. From the south, take Milpas Street exit to Olive and turn right.

Bed, Breakfast and Fantastic Baths
BATH STREET INN
Santa Barbara

The Bath Street Inn occupies an 1873 three-story Queen Anne Victorian with a gabled roof. Innkeepers Susan Brown and Nancy Stover have kept the vintage charm of the place, while rebuilding the rear to focus on the lovely gardens and views of the Santa Ynez Mountains.

Some Victorian overtones remain in the attractive loving room, where tea is served afternoons in front of a big fireplace and leaded-glass doors open to a shady side garden. There is a choice of several spots to enjoy your morning meal of juice, fruits, granola, homemade breads and croissants; a sunny deck and garden behind the house, an intimate breakfast area adjoining the kitchen, or a formal dining room, which seats twelve and is also used for small conferences. Books and flowers are in all the bedrooms. Four rooms occupy the second floor, and three other bedrooms nestle under the top-floor eaves, the beds set in alcoves draped with floral patterns that match the spreads and window curtains. The third floor also has a library and TV room, equipped with love seats, games and puzzles—nothing fancy, but as Susan says, "It's a place where you can relax and put your feet on the table."

The Bath Street Inn should really be classified as a BBB&B: bed, breakfast, bath and bicycles. The baths here are very special, with basins set into Victorian dressers, and two have gigantic claw-footed tubs where you can soak and enjoy a view of the mountains after a bike tour of town. Bicycles are provided, compliments of the house.

BATH STREET INN, 1720 Bath Street, Santa Barbara, California 93101. Telephone: (805) 682-9680. Accommodations: twin, queen- or king-size beds; private baths with tub or stall shower; no telephones; no television. Rates: moderate to expensive, Continental breakfast included. Children over 14 sometimes accepted midweek. No pets. Cards: MC, VISA. Facilities for small conferences. Open all year.

Getting There: Take Carrillo exit off Highway 101 and head east to Bath; turn left.

Showcase for a Designer's Talent
THE BAYBERRY INN
Santa Barbara

Built in 1886, this handsome house was once a girl's boarding school, later a sorority house, and for a while a B&B known as Valerio Manor. Then, in the early 1980s, Keith Pomeroy and interior designer Carlton Wagner bought the place and, over a period of some four years, transformed it into one of the most luxurious little inns in southern California.

Wagner has created a designer's showcase. In the dining room, for example, the walls are covered in silk, the high-backed chairs upholstered with Italian tapestry are from a villa on Lake Como, the carpeting was handwoven in England, and overhead, framed by mirrors, is a ceiling of shirred silk—a Wagner signature. In most of the guest rooms, a canopy of shirred silk surrounds a wreath of berries from which a crystal chandelier hangs over a velvet-draped bed heaped with down pillows. Perfectionism extends to the tiniest details, such as hand-ironed sheets. Many of the bedrooms have fireplaces, too.

The variety of berries in each wreath changes according to the name and theme of the bedroom. Raspberry's wallpaper was handprinted in Paris with *framboises*; Gooseberry has mirrored walls; and Blueberry boasts a bathroom you could give a party in; the tub's on a sun porch decked out with rattan love seats, plants and even refreshments. The only room without a canopy wreath is Thimbleberry: instead, you can gaze at the stars through a skylight over the bed and soak in a deep tub with Jacuzzi jets.

Breakfast is a formal affair at the Bayberry Inn, served on Royal Dalton china with heirloom sterling flatware. It's also a substantial affair, with a main course of omelet or frittata or perhaps a Roquefort soufflé. In the evening, refreshments are served at fireside in the large living room, where multipaned windows look into the garden. Throughout the day, coffee, soft drinks and cookies are available in the enclosed sun porch. And if you want music with your snack here, there's a player piano, too. How about some exercise? You'll find croquet and badminton equipment in the garden and bikes to ride into town.

THE BAYBERRY INN, 111 West Valerio Street, Santa Barbara, California 93101. Telephone: (805) 682-3199. Accommodations: eight rooms with queen-size beds; private baths with tub/shower; telephones in some rooms on request; television on request. Rates: expensive, breakfast included. No children. No pets. No smoking. Cards: AE, MC, VISA. Open all year.

Getting There: From Highway 101 take Mission Street exit, turn right on De la Vina and turn left on Valerio.

In Celebration of the Santa Ynez Valley
THE BALLARD INN
Ballard

The beautiful Santa Ynez Valley, north of Santa Barbara, has long been the headquarters for southern California's horsey set, but today it's also a destination for wine bibbers. Nine small wineries are now located in the area, offering tastings and tours. Other recreational activities include airplane/glider rides, hot-air ballooning, golf, tennis and horseback riding. In the nearby mountains, Cachuma Lake provides facilities for boating and fishing. And for snoopy types, guided tours advertise a peek at the ranch of the area's best-known citizen—Ronald Reagan.

Among the valley's prime tourist attractions are two towns that vividly contrast the Old and the New Worlds. Los Olivos, site of the historic Mattei's Tavern, recalls the Wild West, and Solvang, a re-creation of a Danish village, is a maze of windmills, half-timbered

The Ballard Inn

motels with Scandinavian names, smorgasbord restaurants, gift shops and bakeries. The Mission Santa Inés on the edge of town is the only reminder that this is California.

Between these two towns, amid farms and horse ranches, is Ballard, which contained only a church, a schoolhouse and a general-store-turned-restaurant until the Ballard Inn was built in 1985. Though new, the inn fits into the pastoral picture, looking somewhat like a Victorian farmhouse behind its white picket fence. The interior, though, is sophisticated country elegance at its best, with each of the light-splashed rooms decorated to commemorate persons or events that were significant to the valley's history.

Fifteen guest rooms occupy the second floor, offering views of the countryside through multipaned windows. Seven rooms have fireplaces, and most have handmade patchwork quilts on the beds and interesting little touches of western Americana, such as school desks or old-fashioned sewing machines converted into night tables. Amenities include a welcoming basket of fruit, chocolate and cheese; the bathrooms are stocked with soaps made from wine and with champagne shampoos.

Down a grand staircase are four spacious common rooms, used exclusively by inn guests. A full breakfast is served at individual tables in the handsome dining room, where a fire burns in a large hearth. Besides fresh fruit and juices or frappes, the menu includes entrées like omelets or french toast. In the late afternoon the inn offers wine and a high tea that features such goodies as steak tartare and tiny quiches. You can enjoy this by the fireplace in the elegant drawing room or in the informal game room, where a TV is set up to catch the evening news. It's so comfortable here, you might not want to leave.

THE BALLARD INN, 2436 Baseline, Ballard, California 93463. Telephone: (805) 688-7770. Accommodations: fifteen rooms with twin or queen-size beds; private baths with tub/shower; one room fully equipped for the handicapped; no telephones; no television. Rates: very expensive, breakfast and tea included. No children. No pets. No smoking. Cards: MC, VISA. Facilities for weddings and conferences. Open all year.

Getting There: From San Francisco take Highway 101 to the Los Olivos turnoff five miles north of Buellton; in Los Olivos turn right on Alamo Pintado Road, then turn left on Baseline. From Santa Barbara, take Highway 101 to Buellton, head east on Highway 246 through Solvang, turn left on Alamo Pintado Road and right on Baseline.

UNION HOTEL
Los Alamos

In the sleepy little agricultural town of Los Alamos, Dick Langdon has re-created the spirit of 1880 in the Union Hotel. The original hotel was built of wood that year and served as a Wells Fargo stagecoach stop until it burned down in 1886. In the early 1900s the hotel was reconstructed in Indian adobe and in the 1960s was modernized to remove whatever traces of antiquity were left. When Dick bought the place in 1972, he dismantled twelve old barns and rebuilt the hotel's facade exactly as it appeared in an 1884 photograph. Inside, decades of paint were stripped to reveal the original woodwork and brass, and rooms were papered with colorful Victorian prints.

Dick spent a year traveling the United States to find antiques. In the high-ceilinged downstairs parlor, a pair of two-centuries-old Egyptian burial urns found in Alabama flank an intricately chiseled fireplace mantel from a mansion in Pasadena. A coffee table was constructed from an oak-framed copper bathtub. There's an 1885 Singer sewing machine, along with chandeliers from Lee J. Cobb's home, and the hotel's original safe, blackened on one side from an early shooting. Swinging doors, from a bordello in New Orleans, lead into a saloon with a 150-year-old bar of solid African mahogany.

47

The large dining room contains furnishings and gaslights from a plantation in Mississippi. Tables are set with lace cloths and an array of old chinaware, no two dishes quite alike. Meals are family-style country cooking with recipes derived from a nineteenth-century cookbook: for dinner, tureens of soup, corn bread, platters of beef and country-baked chicken; for breakfast, apple pancakes and sausage or bacon and eggs served with potatoes and cinnamon rolls.

Upstairs, the fifteen rooms contain some beds that could be museum pieces: a two-hundred-year-old Australian brass and cast-iron bedstead with insets of cloisonné, and an original Murphy bed, concealed in a mahogany armoire. Vintage patchwork quilts and crocheted spreads serve as covers, and even the bedside Bibles are circa 1880.

In and out of the hotel, Dick has created a flurry of old-time activity for his guests. An upstairs parlor houses a Brunswick pool table inlaid with ivory. The yard is now an 1880s park, equipped with old-fashioned streetlights and park benches, brick walkways, and (with a nod to the present) a swimming pool, and a Jacuzzi concealed under the floor of a Victorian gazebo. After dinner guests gather in the saloon for ping pong, shuffleboard and complimentary popcorn. And after breakfast each morning guests are shown the sights of Los Alamos in a 1918 touring car.

The area around Los Alamos has its own attractions. Many guests enjoy touring the twenty-two local wineries or taking a picnic basket, prepared by the hotel, to nearby Zaca Lake. Solvang and the Santa Ynez Valley are not far away. And if the 1880s become too much, you can always slip back another century by visiting the area's two missions: La Purisima Concepción and Santa Inés.

UNION HOTEL, 362 Bell Street (P.O. Box 616) Los Alamos, California 93440. Telephone: (805) 928-3838. Accommodations: fifteen rooms with twin, double or king-size beds; some private baths with tub/shower; shared baths with tub or stall shower; no television; no telephones. Rates: moderate to expensive, breakfast included. Open to the public for dinner; full bar service. No children. No pets. No credit cards. Facilities for weddings. Open all year, Friday, Saturday and Sunday only; also open Thanksgiving.

Getting There: Take Los Alamos exit from Highway 101, fourteen miles north of Buellton and seventeen miles south of Santa Maria.

ROSE VICTORIAN INN
Arroyo Grande

When Queen Elizabeth II visited California in 1983, Diana and Ross Cox invited her to be a guest at their Rose Victorian Inn. Her Majesty never slept here, but a framed letter of regret from Buckingham Palace now hangs in the inn. Actually, the queen would have felt quite at home in the surroundings emanating from her great-great-grandmother's era. The towered stick-Eastlake house was built in 1885 for Charles Pitkin, who owned five hundred acres of orchards and farmland in this lush agricultural valley near Pismo Beach. The Coxes have painted the house in four shades of rose and landscaped the grounds with two hundred rose bushes that trail from an arbor and surround a lawn and a large gazebo—a popular spot for weddings.

The only Pitkin possession remaining is a pump organ in the front parlor, while a square rosewood piano, which once belonged to General John Fremont, occupies a place of honor in the sun-splashed rear

parlor. Each of the six bedrooms is named after a variety of rose and decorated accordingly with vivid colors and floral papers. Tropicana, for example, is papered in an orange-and-white pattern and decorated with white wicker and a white quilted spread. The rooms are light and sunny with views of the farmlands and, on clear days, a glimpse of the ocean. In the rear of the gardens, the Coxes have remodeled the old bunkhouse for more rooms, which are smaller and less expensive but do have private baths. The Coxes' next project is converting the carriage house for another four units with sitting areas and private baths.

Breakfast is a sit-down affair in the formal dining room, which is papered with a paisley silk of burgundy and gold and boasts a lovely Italian crystal chandelier. The meal is hearty—eggs Benedict or Florentine or croissants stuffed with meaty fillings, rotated to give variety. A building behind the inn houses a restaurant that is open to the public for dinner and Sunday brunch. A huge century-old mahogany bar from the Gold Country dominates one end of the room. Windows along one wall look out to the rose gardens, and the tables, set with rose-rimmed china, are cheered by a fire from a brick hearth. Dinners include a relish tray, soup, salad, vegetables fresh from the inn's garden and a selection of entrées that range from seafood to steaks grilled over an oak barbecue. Dinner is included in the price of a room here, and the Coxes also throw in preprandial hors d'oeuvres served to inn guests in the parlor. No one has ever complained of hunger at the Rose Victorian Inn.

ROSE VICTORIAN INN, 789 Valley Road, Arroyo Grande, California 93420. Telephone: (805) 481-5566. Accommodations: ten rooms with queen- or king-size beds, some with an additional single; private and shared baths with tub/shower; no telephones; no television. Rates: moderate, breakfast and dinner included. Restaurant open to the public for dinner Thursday through Sunday and for Sunday brunch. Children over 16 welcome; younger children sometimes allowed. No pets. No smoking in main house. Cards: AE, MC, VISA. Facilities for weddings. Open all year.

Getting There: Arroyo Grande is located on Highway 101. From the north, take the Fair Oaks exit, turn right and then turn left on Valley Road. From the south, take the Traffic Way exit, turn left at Fair Oaks and left on Valley Road.

CENTRAL COAST

Hearst Castle Land
Big Sur
The Monterey Peninsula
Santa Cruz

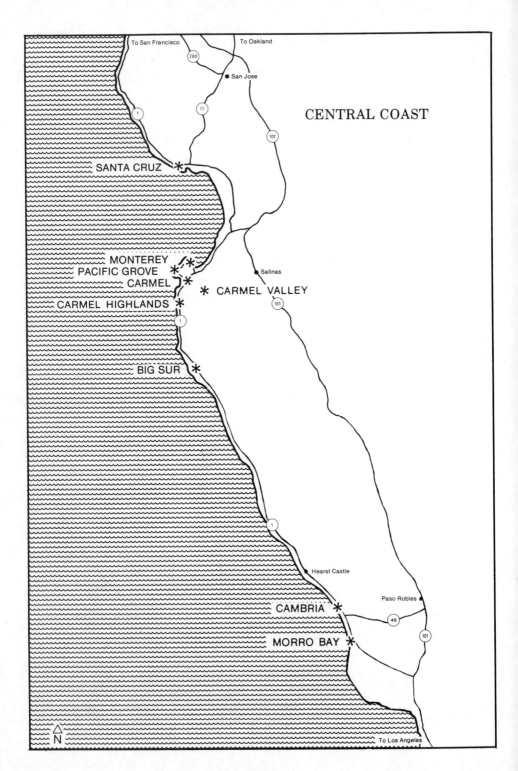

CENTRAL COAST

To San Francisco
To Oakland
280
San Jose
1
17
101
SANTA CRUZ ✶
MONTEREY ✶
PACIFIC GROVE ✶
CARMEL ✶
✶ CARMEL VALLEY
Salinas
101
CARMEL HIGHLANDS ✶
1
BIG SUR ✶
1
Hearst Castle
Paso Robles
CAMBRIA ✶
46
MORRO BAY ✶
101
N
To Los Angeles

52

Enchanted Hills Above the Sea
HEARST CASTLE LAND
From Morro Bay to San Simeon

From the 1920s through the 1940s, publisher William Randolph Hearst devoted a considerable portion of his fortune and energies to creating La Cuesta Encantada, his hilltop estate above the Pacific, midway between Los Angeles and San Francisco. For this fairy-tale castle, he dismantled and reassembled entire rooms and even buildings from Europe, and imported priceless furnishings. Next to the pool is a Grecian temple, and the guest houses are rebuilt French châteaux. For three decades, Hearst and Marion Davies held court at the castle, entertaining notables from Hollywood in particular and the world in general.

In 1958, after Hearst's death, the castle was turned over to the state of California, which operates daily tours for the public. Though Hearst Castle is the area's principal tourist attraction, it is by no means the only reason for visiting this beautiful section of California.

As Highway 1 winds up the coast from the fishing town of Morro Bay, it passes the seaside resort of Cayucos (known for its fine trout and surf fishing, scuba diving and surfing), the quaint hamlet of Harmony (a former creamery converted into a restaurant and shops) and the picturesque village of Cambria (noted for its arts-and-crafts shops and galleries). You'll find good eating along the way.

HEARST CASTLE TOUR TICKETS: Two-hour tours of the castle and grounds depart at least once an hour from eight to three daily, except Thanksgiving, Christmas and New Year's Day. Four itineraries are offered for seeing various parts of the estate, but for first-time visitors, Tour One, which concentrates on the downstairs rooms, is recommended. Reservations are strongly advised and are available from any MISTIX tour agency. Telephone: (800) 446-7275 within California, (619) 452-1950 outside California. Cards: MC, VISA.

Getting There: From Los Angeles, take Highway 101 to San Luis Obispo and Highway 1 north through Morro Bay and Cambria to San Simeon. From San Francisco, take Highway 101 south to Paso Robles, Highway 46 west to the coast and Highway 1 north to San Simeon.

THE INN AT MORRO BAY
Morro Bay

Built at the water's edge, this charming resort overlooking the fishing harbor provides a luxurious base for exploring the Hearst Castle area. The Friden Hotel Company (owner of El Encanto in Santa Barbara) recently renovated this 1950s inn, installed lush gardens and commissioned noted designer Mabel Shultz to redecorate the rooms in French country fashion. The majority of the units have private decks or patios and sweeping views of the bay; many have fireplaces, too, and one suite has a large private Jacuzzi.

From the glass-walled dining room and deck, you are treated to an aerial ballet by the seagulls flying over the harbor; their movements seem to follow the beat of the classical music piped throughout the inn. Birds of all kinds play an important role at Morro Bay. The inn is located next to a wildlife sanctuary that's a bird-watchers' paradise. More active forms of recreation include golf at an adjacent eighteen-hole course, swimming in the inn's pool and bicycling in the surrounding area. In addition to excursions to Hearst Castle, winery touring and tastings are popular diversions. The shops and restaurants of San Luis Obispo are also a short drive away.

THE INN AT MORRO BAY, Morro Bay, California 93442. Telephone: (805) 772-5651, in California (800) 321-9566. Accommodations: one hundred rooms with two double, queen- or king-size beds; private baths; telephones; television. Rates: moderate to very expensive, no meals included. Dining room open to the public for breakfast, lunch and dinner; full bar service. Children welcome. Pets discouraged. Cards: AE, CB, DC, MC, VISA. Facilities for conferences and weddings. Open all year.

Getting There: From Highway 1, take Main Street exit at Morro Bay and follow Main south through the gates of the state park. The inn is on the right.

Log Cabin in the Pines
THE J. PATRICK HOUSE
Cambria

The B&B craze arrived surprisingly late in artsy-craftsy Cambria. In fact, there were none here in the early 1980s when Molly Lynch came to Cambria from southern California to open an inn. She purchased a two-story house built of pine logs on a woodsy hill above the village and, behind it, constructed another two-story unit for seven guest rooms. Molly named the inn after her father, J. Patrick Lynch, whose family came from County Cork, and gave the rooms Irish names like Limerick and Donegal.

The pine walls are exposed in the homey living room, where a brick fireplace sits on a raised hearth. Here, and elsewhere in the inn, you'll find lots of books and magazines, along with comfortable couches and chairs in which to curl up and read them. In the rear breakfast area four tables, set with crocheted cloths and blue china, look into the garden. Molly bakes the morning breads, which are served with fresh fruit and granola.

The bedrooms have the same Early American country look, with lots of knotty pine and flowery wallpapers, beds lavishly piled with pillows, and wood-burning fireplaces. The inn is surrounded by pines and is only minutes away from the beach or village.

THE J. PATRICK HOUSE, 2990 Burton Drive, Cambria, California 93428. Telephone: (805) 927-3812. Accommodations: seven rooms with twin or queen-size beds; private baths with stall shower or tub/shower; no telephones; no television. Rates: moderate, breakfast included. No children. No pets. No smoking. Cards: MC, VISA. Open all year.

Getting There: From Highway 1, turn east on Burton, which is between the two main exits to Cambria.

BEACH HOUSE
Cambria

Moonstone Beach, rimmed by a row of ocean-view motels, is one of Cambria's newest and nicest areas for lodgings. Amid these motels, but set off by surrounding fields, is the Beach House, a pretty little B&B. This inn is a family affair, owned by Penny and Tom Hitch, who live nearby; their six grown children and Penny's mother all help run the place.

Presently, a Continental breakfast and evening refreshments are served in a downstairs sitting room with a breakfast bar and stone fireplace; there's a rear patio with tables, too. But in the near future, the Hitches plan to create a common room in what is now a spacious upstairs area with a cathedral ceiling, a large fireplace and a magnificent ocean view.

The bedroom furnishings are simple, befitting a beach house: down quilts and ruffled pillows atop queen-size beds, circa-1890 oak dressers (from a hotel in Vermont). Most of the rooms have ocean views and all have private baths. The best lodging to be had here, though, is in a second-floor room with a king-size bed, pitched knotty-pine ceiling, skylights and an ocean view; from the private deck, you can glimpse the ornate bell towers of Hearst Castle just six miles away.

BEACH HOUSE, 6360 Moonstone Beach Drive, Cambria, California 93428. Telephone: (805) 927-3136. Accommodations: seven rooms with queen- or king-size beds; private baths; no telephones; television with HBO. Rates: moderate to expensive, Continental breakfast included. Children welcome, but room occupancy is limited to two persons. No pets. No smoking. Cards: MC, VISA. Open all year.

Getting There: From the north, take Moonstone Beach Drive west off Highway 1. From the south, turn left on Windsor Boulevard and right on Moonstone Beach Drive.

Total Luxury and a Spectacular Site
VENTANA INN
Big Sur

Between San Simeon, where Hearst built his castle, and Monterey, the Santa Lucia Mountains rise precipitously above the incessantly pounding Pacific surf. Today Highway 1 traverses this rugged terrain across high bridges and along niches blasted out of the cliffs. The Spanish missionaries found this section of the coast impassable and detoured inland. But this very remoteness appealed to one of the first settlers, a Yankee sea captain with the unlikely name of Juan Bautista Roger Cooper who landed his cargoes at the mouth of Big Sur River to avoid paying customs duties to the Mexicans in Monterey. The struggles of the homesteaders who later tried to farm this land inspired the poetry of Robinson Jeffers. But it was another writer who shaped the destiny of Big Sur. Henry Miller moved here in 1944, seeking the serenity of the coastal mountains after his expatriate days in Paris. Other artists followed, and for the next decade or so Big Sur was a hardworking bohemian community.

Only recently has the traveler to Big Sur been able to sleep in style. In 1975, the Ventana Inn was built on a meadow twelve hundred feet above the Pacific. The contemporary architecture is spectacular, with soaring ceilings, giant beams, unexpected angles and planes. From every room there are views of the mountains, the meadow or the ocean far below. The rooms are paneled with knotty cedar and handsomely appointed with wicker furniture, hand-painted headboards, patchwork quilts and window seats tucked into alcoves. All have private balconies or patios and some have Franklin stoves and individual hot tubs. Two-story units have wet bars and living rooms.

A fire in the lobby helps remove the chill from the morning fogs that often shroud the Santa Lucia range. Here guests receive a light breakfast: freshly squeezed orange juice, breads and pastries from Ventana's own bakery, assorted fruits and coffee. In the afternoon wine and cheese are served. Across the meadow on another hilltop is the Ventana restaurant, which offers a diverse selection of lunch and dinner dishes, as well as fifty-mile vistas from its patio.

There is a large swimming pool at Ventana, plus Japanese hot baths, a sauna and a Jacuzzi. There are hiking trails in the mountains above, and down the road is Nepenthe, a restaurant and bar of intriguing design, built around a cabin that Orson Welles once bought for Rita Hayworth (although they never lived there). Today on a sunny afternoon the broad deck is crowded with locals and visitors sipping wine or beer while enjoying the recorded classical music and a breathtaking view of the coast.

VENTANA INN, Big Sur, California 93920. Telephone: (408) 667-2331, in California (800) 628-6500. Accommodations: forty rooms with queen-size, two queens or king-size beds; private baths with tub/shower, wheelchair access; telephones; television. Rates: very expensive, Continental breakfast included. Restaurant open to the public for lunch and dinner, full bar service. Children discouraged. No pets. Cards: AE, DC, MC, VISA. Open all year.

Getting There: From San Francisco, follow directions to Monterey and take Highway 1 twenty-eight miles south. From Los Angeles, take Highway 101 to San Luis Obispo and Highway 1 north. The inn is south of the village of Big Sur and just north of Nepenthe.

Rich in History and Scenic Beauty
MONTEREY PENINSULA
Monterey, Carmel and Pacific Grove

In 1770 Father Junipero Serra founded Mission San Carlos in Monterey, the second in California's chain of missions. The following year he moved the mission to Carmel, and later returned here to spend his last years. The Spanish military expedition that Serra accompanied had established a presidio in Monterey. In 1775 Spain designated Monterey as the capital of California, and so it remained through the Mexican rule until the American flag was raised over the Customhouse in 1846.

Monterey had become a cultivated town, where the Spanish citizens and their families lived auspiciously in two-story adobe casas with roofs of red tile. Then the Yankees discovered the abundance of whales offshore and turned this sedate Spanish community into a bustling whaling port. Sardine fishing brought added prosperity and west of town, Cannery Row was built and later immortalized in the works of John Steinbeck. Today many of the old adobes are open to the public or house restaurants and shops. And after the sardines had all but disappeared, Cannery Row was converted into a complex of shops, hotels and dining places.

Steinbeck was not the only writer beguiled by this lovely peninsula. Robert Louis Stevenson lived in Monterey in 1879. Then after the turn of the century a group of writers and artists settled in Carmel. Edward Weston, Maynard Dixon, Ambrose Bierce, Don Blanding, Lincoln Steffens and Robinson Jeffers also lived here over the years. Although Carmel is built in a potpourri of architectural styles—from Victorian and half-timbered cottage to neo-Spanish—new construction or remodeling is strictly controlled to preserve the woodsy, village-like quality of the picturesque streets.

Pacific Grove is vastly different from Monterey and Carmel. Founded in the 1870s by the Methodist Church to the west of Monterey, the town became known as the Chautauqua of the West, famous for its summertime religious conferences, an educational tradition that's kept alive today at the Asilomar Conference grounds. The city's streets and its rocky coast are lined with large Victorians that were built to house the conference attendees and, later, as the town gained favor as a summer resort, vacationers. Today many of these stately old mansions are being converted into inns, and with a growing number of good restaurants and shops, Pacific Grove is again making a strong bid for the tourist business.

Few places in the West offer such diverse recreational facilities as the Monterey Peninsula. There are eight public and four private golf courses. Sailboats may be chartered in Monterey Bay. Skin diving, scuba diving, fishing, tennis, polo matches—they're all here. Then there is the spectacular shoreline to explore, from the cypress-bordered white sand dunes of Carmel to the rocky coves and hidden beaches of Lovers Point. Carmel is a shopper's paradise with a plethora of crafts, jewelry, clothing and antique stores. It's a sightseer's mecca, too, with choices that include reliving history at the old mission or viewing the palatial mansions along Pebble Beach's famed Seventeen-Mile Drive. The Monterey Peninsula probably has more restaurants per capita than any other area of the West. And the latest attraction, for some two million people each year, is the spectacular Monterey Bay Aquarium.

Getting There: From San Francisco take Highway 101 to the Monterey Peninsula cutoff, north of Salinas; in Castroville this joins Highway 1, which goes through Monterey to Carmel. For a longer and more scenic route from San Francisco, take Highway 280 to San Jose, Highway 17 through Los Gatos to Santa Cruz, and Highway 1 south to Monterey. From Los Angeles, take Highway 101 to Salinas and Highway 68 to Monterey.

OLD MONTEREY INN
Monterey

When Ann and Gene Swett decided to open their elegant Tudor-style home for bed and breakfast, they vowed they would make it the perfect inn. And they have succeeded, down to every detail. Built in 1929 by Carmel Martin, a former mayor of Monterey, the half-timbered house sits on an oak-studded hillside surrounded by an acre of beautiful gardens. Begonias, fuschias and hydrangeas abound, along with twenty-eight varieties of roses. The wooded banks of a creek are rampant with ivy, ferns and rhododendrons.

The interior of the house (where the Swetts raised six children, now grown and gone) is decorated with impeccable taste. Bedrooms are equipped with comfortable places to sit—wicker chairs or upholstered love seats or perhaps a chaise—and with books and magazines to read. Plants and well-chosen pieces of bric-a-brac make the house look homey but not cluttered. Bathrooms are well stocked with bubble bath and essentials you might have left at home, like toothpaste and razor blades. Downstairs a large refrigerator is filled with soft drinks and fruit juices, compliments of the house, and a pot of coffee is always ready.

Wood-burning fireplaces enhance most of the ten bedrooms. The most spectacular of these is the Library, which has floor-to-ceiling shelves of books, and a private balcony with a chaise. A king-size bed occupies a niche with windows on all sides. There is no need for window shades here; the limbs of a massive gnarled oak provide all the privacy you need. On the third floor, tucked under the eaves, are two enchanting rooms with fireplaces, half-timbered walls, and skylights in the slanted ceilings. And behind the inn is another fireplace unit: a two-room shuttered cottage dressed up in plaid and flowered patterns of lime and green. A sitting room with a dramatic skylight is furnished with wicker ware; up a few steps is a cozy bedroom with a window seat overlooking the garden.

In the evenings a fire also burns in the lovely high-ceilinged living room, where predinner refreshments are served. A table is set up for backgammon or dominoes. And to help you choose from the peninsula's many restaurants, there's a book in which previous guests have written critiques of their local dining experiences. In the morning you may have a breakfast tray brought to your room, or you may join the other guests in the formally appointed dining room beside yet another fire. Breakfast starts with a glass of orange juice and a plate of fresh fruit, followed by

Old Monterey Inn

the inn's now-famous cheese puffs and popovers. Recently the Swetts have started serving a hot dish, such as quiche or Belgian waffles with sautéed pears.

In fact, every time you return to this inn, you'll find more improvements. At this writing the "perfect inn" seemed quite perfect. But the Swetts were adding a small sitting room with fireplace to one of the bedrooms, and in another unit, a claw-legged tub will be replaced with a whirlpool bath. Perfection, evidently, knows no end.

OLD MONTEREY INN, 500 Martin Street, Monterey, California 93940. Telephone: (408) 375-8284. Accommodations: ten rooms with queen- or king-size beds; private baths with tub/shower or shower only; no telephones; no television. Rates: expensive to very expensive, breakfast included. No children. No pets. No smoking. No credit cards. Open all year.

Getting There: Take Munras exit off of Highway 1 and turn left on Soledad Drive. Turn right on Pacific and turn left on Martin Street.

Tulgey Wood, Borogrove and Bay Views Too
THE JABBERWOCK
Monterey

Razzleberry flabjous might be on the morning menu and you'll sleep in room called Tulgey Wood or Borogrove with views of the garden or Monterey Bay. All this nonsense comes from The Jabberwock poem in *Alice in Wonderland.* But you won't need a looking glass to enjoy this place, though the binoculars or telescopes placed in the view rooms do help you spot the seals and sea otters that bark in the bay. This towered and turreted house on the hillside four blocks above Cannery Row was built in 1911, served as a Catholic convent for fifty years and later was the headquarters for the local Church of Scientology, before Jim and Barbara Allen bought it for an inn in 1982. They chose the name Jabberwock because Jim loved the sound of it. "When I was a kid, that's the only poem I ever learned," he admits.

The charming guest rooms are decorated with flowered papers, antique furniture, goose-down quilts and ruffled pillows, on which a handmade sachet of potpourri is placed. Bathrobes are thoughtfully provided in case you left yours at home. The Toves, a downstairs bedroom, has an especially striking headboard and matching dresser of burled walnut and opens to a private brick patio, while Borogrove offers the best view, along with a fireplace and sitting area. Two garret rooms share a sitting area with a bay view that extends all the way to Santa Cruz.

There are plenty of other places to relax in, however: a homey living room cheered by a brick fireplace, a glassed-in veranda with comfortable rattan chairs for reading and tables for puzzles or games, or the garden, filled with ferns, roses, begonias, dahlias and iris. A big Continental breakfast is served at fireside in the dining room with Jabberwock names for the day's dish etched in reverse on glass. At five o'clock a bell bids you to gather with other guests for refreshments. At any time of night or day you may help yourself to complimentary soft drinks from a refrigerator dubbed "The Tum Tum Tree." And when you retire with cookies, milk and a Lewis Carroll volume on the bedside table, you'll truly think you are in Wonderland.

THE JABBERWOCK, 598 Laine Street, Monterey, California 93940. Telephone: (408) 372-4777. Accommodations: seven rooms with queen- or king-size beds; three rooms have private baths with showers; others share two baths with tub/shower and shower; no telephones; no television. Rates: expensive, breakfast included. Smoking restricted to sun porch. No credit cards. No younger children. No pets. Open all year.

Getting There: From San Francisco take Del Monte Avenue off Highway 1 into Monterey, following signs to Cannery Row through the tunnel to Lighthouse Avenue. Turn left on Hoffman to Laine, and turn left again. From Carmel take the Munras Avenue exit off of Highway 1, turn left on Soledad and right on Pacific Street which leads to Lighthouse Avenue. Pick-up service at Monterey airport by advance arrangement.

Sleep by the Surf in a Sea of Down
SPINDRIFT INN
Monterey

Resorts once dotted the beaches west of Monterey, until the sardine industry claimed the area for its canneries. Now the pendulum has swung full circle and Cannery Row—with its many shops, hotels and restaurants—is again a mecca for vacationers. Steinbeck would not recognize his old turf, but even he might think the Spindrift Inn, on the edge of the bay, was a survivor of the last century. From the outside it looks that way. The old-fashioned facade, however, conceals one of the newest and most luxurious small hotels in all of California.

When you enter the elegant lobby, you leave behind the hurly-burly of Cannery Row. If it's late afternoon, tea will be served by the marble-faced fireplace, flanked by gilded statues holding giant candelabras. Sun splashes in from a skylight over the four-story atrium above the lobby. And an elevator will whisk you up to a lovely room with gleaming hardwood floors, Oriental rugs, European period furnishings and window seats from which you can view the bay or the hills of Monterey through multipaned glass.

At night you will snuggle up in a sea of down pillows and comforters atop a feather bed. A wood fire burns in the hearth and, from the oceanside rooms, you can hear the surf breaking on the beach below. Romantic, yes. But if you're not in the mood, just press a bedside button to catch the latest Home Box Office movies on the TV, concealed in an armoire. In the morning, you will be brought a silver tray laden with freshly squeezed orange juice, fruit, pastries and a rose.

The Spindrift Inn is but a short walk from the new aquarium and the many sights of Cannery Row. But you might just want to spend your day loafing on a chaise in the flower-bedecked roof garden with its 360-degree view of the ocean, bay and Monterey.

SPINDRIFT INN, 652 Cannery Row, Monterey, California 93940. Telephone: (408) 646-8900, in California (800) 841-1879, nationwide (800) 225-2901. Accommodations: forty-two rooms with two double, queen- or king-size beds; private baths with tub/shower, some with sauna; some rooms fully equipped for the handicapped; telephones; television. Rates: very expensive, Continental breakfast included. Children welcome. No pets. Cards: AE, CB, DC, MC, VISA. Open all year.

Getting There: From San Francisco take Del Monte Avenue exit off Highway 1 into Monterey and follow signs to Cannery Row. From Carmel take the Munras Avenue exit off Highway 1, turn left on Soledad, right on Pacific and follow signs to Cannery Row.

A Fairy-Tale Setting on Monterey Bay

THE GREEN GABLES INN
Pacific Grove

The advent of the railway to Pacific Grove brought affluent vacationers who erected elaborate homes along the craggy coast of Monterey Bay. One of these showplaces—a half-timbered mansion of many gables— was built in 1888 by William Lacy, who sold it shortly thereafter to a judge from Monterey seeking a summer home. Roger and Sally Post (owners of The Gosby House) have transformed this handsome residence and an adjacent carriage house into one of the area's most exquisite inns.

It's a dazzling setting with breathtaking views of the water and mountains beyond, glimpsed from windows, which are crafted in a myriad of sizes and shapes into a seemingly endless number of alcoves, dormers and bays. From window seats or love seats in the upstairs bedrooms you can watch the sea otters at play, the seals sunning on rocks that protrude from the bay, or occasionally a passing whale. But the most spectacular feature of these rooms are the sloping beamed ceilings that pitch every which way. One of the rooms, originally a chapel, is entered through a quadruple set of carved doors and distinguished by a stunning rib-vaulted ceiling. The Posts have appointed the guest rooms generously: soft quilts and a plethora of pillows on the beds, antique writing tables, bowls of fruit, plants, books and magazines. Only two bedrooms have private baths, but a caddy of soap and towels, plus robes, are provided for those that share. On the lower floor, there's a two-room suite with a fireplace edged with Delft tiles and a sofa that makes up into an extra bed.

More alcoves and bays embellish the living room, where a fireplace rimmed with stained glass soars to a twelve-foot ceiling, which is bordered by a sculptured frieze, painted bright blue. In the dining room a crystal chandelier is suspended from a graceful medallion over a formal table. There's a fireplace here, too, and a dramatic view through

Green Gables Inn

windows framed with latticework. A sit-down breakfast combines a substantial main course—crêpes or Belgian waffles or frittata—with fresh fruits, juices, granola and muffins.

A patio behind the house is planted with azaleas and impatiens. Beyond that a carriage house contains four more rooms. These don't have the fairy-tale ambience of the main house, but they do provide more privacy, along with fireplaces, television and modern baths.

THE GREEN GABLES INN, 104 Fifth Street, Pacific Grove, California 93950. Telephone: (408) 375-2095. Accommodations: ten rooms with double and queen-size beds, some with trundle beds; two rooms with tub or shower, carriage house rooms have private baths with stall shower; no telephones; television in some rooms. Rates: expensive, breakfast included. Children permitted in carriage house only. No pets. Cards: AE, MC, VISA. Open all year.

Getting There: From Highway 1 take Highway 68 west to Pacific Grove, continue on Forest Avenue to Ocean View Boulevard, then turn right to Fifth Street.

The House That Never Stops Growing
THE GOSBY HOUSE INN
Pacific Grove

In the days when Pacific Grove was a major stopping point on the Chautauqua circuit, many Victorian lodging houses were built around the town. One of these was originally constructed in a rather simple style by J. F. Gosby in 1887. But as his guest register grew, so did the house—in both size and architectural complexity. The large Queen Anne tower that now distinguishes the house was built to spite his neighbor, who had built an intricately ornamented Queen Anne next door.

These traditions of hospitality, improvement and growth have been carried on by the Gosby's present owners, Roger and Sally Post. After an extensive renovation, they opened the inn in 1977 and have never stopped improving it. Over the years more units (two with kitchens and fireplaces) were added in rear buildings opening to a pretty garden, and the interior was overhauled to provide private baths and fireplaces in most of the rooms.

The Gosby's rooms are designed in turn-of-the-century style with flowered wallpapers, antique furniture and ruffled muslin curtains.

The Carriage House at the Gosby House

Bowls of fruit and fresh flowers are placed in the rooms. There's always a gracious innkeeper (in old-fashioned attire) on duty to brew a cup of tea or chocolate any time of the day or help you with restaurant reservations or sightseeing plans. Hot spiced cider and hors d'oeuvres are served in the evening and a full breakfast is served in the morning—either in the parlor or in an adjoining meeting and game room with a fireplace. And when you retire, there's another touch of Gosby hospitality: a turned-down bed with an imported chocolate and a flower on the pillow.

THE GOSBY HOUSE INN, 643 Lighthouse Avenue, Pacific Grove, California 93950. Telephone: (408) 375-1287. Accommodations: twenty-two rooms with double, two double, or queen-size beds; private baths with tub/shower or stall shower in all but two rooms, which share bath; wheelchair access; telephones; no television. Rates: expensive, breakfast included. Children permitted in some rooms. No pets. Smoking restricted to certain guest rooms. Cards: AE, MC, VISA. Open all year.

Getting There: From Highway 1, take the Pebble Beach/17-Mile Drive turnoff. Turn right onto Highway 68, which leads to Pacific Grove. Turn left at Lighthouse Avenue and proceed three blocks to the inn.

Echoes of a Literary Past
THE STONEHOUSE INN
Carmel

Among those who nourished Carmel as an artists' colony was an expatriate San Franciscan known as Nana Foster. In 1906 she built a house of hand-hewn stone on the sand dunes above the beach and invited the prominent writers of the era to be her guests. Today the inn's bedrooms bear the names of some of the literati who stayed there—Jack London, Mary Austin and others who were most likely visitors as well, such as Robinson Jeffers and Sinclair Lewis. Even though the view of the ocean is obscured by the houses and trees that now surround the inn, the feeling of early Carmel remains.

Literary ghosts, however, are not the only inhabitants of this charming retreat. Teddy bears and flocks of stuffed, ceramic and wooden ducks occupy nearly every nook and cranny of the large living room and the cozy glassed-in sun porch. They even march up the stairs to the four guest rooms that nestle under the gabled and dormered roof. These and all other rooms throughout the house have the white-painted board-and-batten walls so typical of early Carmel houses. They are appointed with antiques, quilted spreads, ruffled curtains, a bevy of pillows, silk flowers and bowls of fruit. Downstairs are two other bedrooms, one with its own porch.

A sit-down breakfast is served in the tile-floored dining room where multipaned windows on three sides look into gardens and foliage. Innkeeper Virginia Carey usually provides fruits, juices, a hot entrée and homemade breads. Coffee, tea and hot chocolate are offered all day. And in late afternoon more refreshments and hors d'oeuvres are served beside the enormous stone fireplace in the living room where the literary elite of yesteryear used to gather. If those stones could only talk.

THE STONEHOUSE INN, Eighth below Monte Verde (P.O. Box 2517), Carmel, California 93921. Telephone: (408) 624-4569. Accommodations: six rooms with twin, double, queen- and king-size beds; three shared baths, tub/shower or stall shower; no telephones; no television. Rates: moderate, breakfast included. Children over 14 welcome. No pets. No smoking. Cards: MC, VISA. Open all year.

Getting There: Off Ocean Avenue turn south on Monte Verde. Turn right on Eighth.

SEA VIEW INN
Carmel

The Sea View has been operated as an inn since the mid-1920s, but Marshall and Diane Hydorn, the present owners, think the three-story shingled house was probably built just after the turn of the century. They also like to think it was designed by Bernard Maybeck, as one book on Carmel history suggests. Located three blocks from the ocean on a quiet residential street, the inn was obviously named for its view; however, over the years large pines have grown up around the house, allowing only a peek at the sea from upstairs rooms today.

The inn retains the aura of Carmel in the twenties, even though the Hydorns recently redecorated the rooms in a sophisticated country style. Downstairs, the dark beamed ceilings of the parlor and library contrast with white board-and-batten walls and shuttered windows. Navy blue love seats are pulled up in front of the fireplace in the parlor and, in the library, a backgammon board is set by another fire. Breakfast is served here, *by candlelight,* and what a repast it is. On weekends the menu is usually quiche and sausage, four cereals, freshly baked apple or date bread, croissants, seasonal fruits and cheeses; on weekdays, however, the fare is simpler.

Many of the second-floor bedrooms have sitting areas in alcoves or enclosed porches and shuttered window seats in bays. Canopies of floral fabrics adorn the beds and handsome area rugs grace the polished oak floors. The cozy garret rooms on the top floor are done up in Victorian wicker, braided rugs and flowery prints. Throughout plants abound along with the paintings of Marshall Hydorn. Seaview is a romantic place with a loyal clientele. It is not uncommon these days for couples who had honeymooned here to return for their fiftieth anniversies.

SEA VIEW INN, Camino Real at Eleventh (P.O. Box 4138), Carmel, California 93921. Telephone: (408) 624-8778. Accommodations: eight rooms with queen- or king-size beds; private or shared baths with tub/shower or shower only; no telephones; no television. Rates: moderate, breakfast included. Children over 12 welcome. No pets. No smoking. Cards: MC, VISA. Open all year.

Getting There: From Ocean Avenue, turn south on Camino Real.

A Poetic Flower-Filled Hideaway
VAGABOND HOUSE
Carmel

Don Blanding lived here in the 1940s, but no one is certain if his poem "Vagabond's House" was named for the inn, or if the inn was named for the poem. Nevertheless Vagabond House is a poetic hideaway with rooms looking through treetops into a stone courtyard filled with rhododendrons, camelias, azaleas and roses. In the center, baskets of ferns, begonias and fuchsias hang from the branches of a large oak.

Vagabond House was originally built in 1941 for efficiency apartments when Carmel's population suddenly swelled from the influx of military personnel to Fort Ord. Later it became an inn and is presently owned by Dennis and Karen Levett. The rooms are large and charmingly furnished with Early American maple, pieces of wicker, quilted bedspreads, antique pendulum clocks, books and flowers. Most of the rooms have fireplaces and all have refrigerators or kitchenettes, a holdover from apartment house days.

Off the patio is a large common room with a fireplace and a collection of English hunt prints. A substantial buffet breakfast is laid out here in the mornings: freshly squeezed orange juice, muffins and currant rolls with strawberry jam, a fruit basket and hard-cooked eggs. (If you prefer, a phone call will bring a breakfast tray to your room.) No one goes hungry here, even the squirrels. A big sack of peanuts is provided so you can feed the friendly little creatures that congregate on the patio and window ledge.

The Levetts also own Lincoln Green Inn, a group of four cottages set among gardens on the far side of town near the Carmel River. Each has a living room with fireplace, separate bedroom and full kitchen. There is no common room or food service at Lincoln Green, but guests are welcome to take their breakfast at Vagabond House. Reservations may also be made through Vagabond House.

VAGABOND HOUSE, Fourth and Dolores (P.O. Box 2747), Carmel, California 93921. Telephone: (408) 624-7738. Accommodations: twelve rooms with two doubles, queen- or king-size beds; private baths, some with tub/shower, some with shower only; telephones; color television. Rates: moderate to expensive, breakfast included. No children under 12. No pets. Cards: AE, MC, VISA. Open all year.

Getting There: From Ocean Avenue turn north on Dolores. Free pickup at Monterey Airport.

Vagabond House

Privacy and the Sound of the Surf

SAN ANTONIO HOUSE

Carmel

This three-story shingled house was built in 1907 as a private residence, and during its early years served as a studio and weekend retreat for artists and writers from the San Francisco Bay Area. In the 1930s Lincoln Steffens lived next door and played host to a continuous flow of the literati of his day. In 1950, the handsome old house, set back from the street by a spacious lawn, became a guest house. It is presently owned by Vagabond House proprietors Dennis and Karen Levett. The accommodations consist of two- and three-room suites, each with its own patio or garden. All of the units have fireplaces, one suite has a full kitchen and the others have refrigerators. In the morning, the newspaper is at your door and when you're ready for breakfast, just pick up the phone. The resident innkeeper will bring you a tray laden with the same goodies that are served at Vagabond House. San Antonio House is a place for people who seek complete privacy and the sound of the surf. It's only a block away from Carmel's beautiful beach.

SAN ANTONIO HOUSE, San Antonio between Seventh and Ocean (P.O. Box 3683), Carmel, California 93921. Telephone: (408) 624-4334. Accommodations: queen-size beds; private baths with tub/shower; telephones; color television. Rates: expensive, breakfast included. No children under 12. Cards: AE, MC, VISA. Open all year.

Getting There: Take Ocean Avenue to San Antonio and turn south.

San Antonio House

SANDPIPER INN-AT-THE-BEACH
Carmel

Graeme and Irene Mackenzie, who bought the Sandpiper Inn in 1975, are no starry-eyed novices to the tasks of innkeeping. Rarely will you encounter a small inn managed so professionally. Born in Scotland, Mackenzie graduated from Lausanne Hotel School and did post-graduate work at Cornell University. He brings to Carmel over twenty years of experience in some of the finest hotels in Europe, Bermuda, Hong Kong, the United States and Canada.

The Sandpiper Inn, located on Carmel Point just fifty yards from the beach, has been in operation since 1929. The Mackenzies completely refurbished it, adding many antiques: a mixture of American country, French and English pieces. Quilted flowered spreads cover the new king- and queen-size beds, and bowls of fresh flowers are on the tables. Some of the rooms have wood-burning fireplaces and many have views of Carmel Bay and Pebble Beach. The Mackenzies added full modern baths to all of the fifteen rroms and rebuilt two small cottages behind the inn.

George Washington never slept here, nor did any other American president, but Graeme Mackenzie jokingly points to a bed that President Ford slept in while staying at a home in Pebble Beach. There was no king-size bed in the guest room, but the Sandpiper graciously lent one of theirs for Ford's comfort.

The Mackenzies' guest book, however, does list the presidents of many corporations, along with an international clientele representing sixty-six countries. In the evening, around the stone fireplace in the spacious living room, you are likely to hear many languages. Graeme and Irene are both multilingual, (she is a former United Nations interpreter), which helps the foreign visitors feel at home.

To one side of the living room is a cozy library with a writing desk and shelves stocked with books. At the end of the living room is a long table where a breakfast of orange juice, hot Danish pastries and coffee is served. Guests are invited to help themselves to coffee in the kitchen at any time.

Flower gardens surround the inn, with brick patios for sunning. Ten-speed bicycles are available for peddling along the cypress-studded drive that fronts Carmel's glorious beach. Graeme is happy to suggest restaurants and tours of the excellent Monterey County

Sandpiper Inn-at-the-Beach

wineries and to introduce guests to most of the famous golf and tennis clubs on the peninsula.

SANDPIPER INN-AT-THE-BEACH, 2408 Bay View Avenue at Martin, Carmel, California 93923. Telephone: (408) 624-6433. Accommodations: fifteen rooms with queen- or king-size beds with an additional single bed in some rooms; private baths with tub/shower or shower only; no telephones; television in living room. Rates: moderate to expensive. Continental breakfast included. Children over 12 welcome. No pets. Cards: MC, VISA. Open all year.

Getting There: Take Ocean Avenue to Scenic Avenue and proceed south along the beach to the end; seventy yards beyond the stop sign in the middle of the road, turn left at Martin.

A Sun-Blessed Sanctuary for Golfers

QUAIL LODGE
Carmel Valley

The Carmel Valley Golf and Country Club is spread over 245 exquisitely landscaped acres, studded with ten pretty lakes, lovely gardens and an eighteen-hole golf course. The jewel in its crown is Quail Lodge, a luxurious resort that offers its guests full privileges of the country club facilities.

Some fifty years ago, all this was but a dream to the club's developer, Ed Haber, who in the 1930s won San Francisco's amateur golf championship and aspired to build his own course one day. Nearly four decades were to pass before Haber's dream was fulfilled. He bought a dairy farm in the Carmel Valley from Dwight Morrow, brother of Ann Morrow Lindbergh, and transformed it into the present club and resort.

The hub of Quail Lodge is a handsome contemporary building overlooking one of the lakes. In the main lobby a skylight is embedded in the high ceiling to illuminate a fountain below. Coffee, tea and sherry are served here in the afternoons, and you may enjoy your refreshments by the fireplaces in the adjoining library or sun room, while admiring the view of the lake. The central lodge also houses The Covey, an elegant, award-winning restaurant.

The ninety-six guest rooms are located in fifteen smaller buildings scattered through the grounds on either side of the main lodge. All have garden or lake views and private decks or balconies. The most desirable accommodations are the cottage suites, where the bedroom opens to a large, high-ceilinged living room with a fireplace and a wet bar completely stocked with just about everything you might want to drink. Four single rooms also occupy each of these cottages and, when a group is traveling together, all may share the amenities of the living area.

Even if you're not a golfer, you'll find plenty of activity at Quail Lodge: hot tubs, swimming pools, a croquet court, and jogging and cycling trails, as well as steelhead fishing (in season) on the Carmel River, which winds through the grounds. You'll also find year-round trout fishing and boating on a four-acre lake in a contiguous six-hundred acres recently acquired by the resort. And on most days throughout the year, you can be assured of sunny weather for this outdoors life. Smart travelers know that the sun shines in Carmel Valley when the rest of the Monterey area is shrouded in fog.

QUAIL LODGE, 8205 Valley Greens Drive, Carmel, California 93923. Telephone: (408) 624-1581, for reservations only in California (800) 682-9303, nationwide (800) 538-9516. Accommodations: ninety-six units with one king-size or two queen-size beds; private baths with tub/shower; telephones; television. Rates: very expensive, no meals included. The Covey restaurant open to the public for dinner; Carmel Valley Golf and Country Club open to lodge guests for breakfast and lunch, shuttle service provided; full bar service. Children welcome. No pets. Cards: AE, CB, DC, MC, VISA. Conference facilities. Open all year.

Getting There: From Highway 1, just south of the Ocean Avenue turnoff to Carmel, head east on Carmel Valley Road until you see the Quail Lodge sign on the right.

On the Pacific's Edge

HIGHLANDS INN

Carmel Highlands

This cluster of shingled buildings clings to a pine-studded hillside that rises abruptly from the Pacific south of Carmel. Highlands Inn, with 146 rooms, is larger than most hostelries in this book, but none can surpass it for its spectacular view and world-class accommodations.

The present Highlands Inn is a reincarnation of a rustic lodge, surrounded by cabins, that was built in 1916. The lodge, constructed of locally quarried golden granite, was renovated in the early 1980s. Skylights now brighten the enormous common room with its two huge stone fireplaces. And a wall of glass on the ocean side (where the cocktail lounge and Pacific's Edge restaurant are located) provides awesome views of the Pacific framed by the craggy fingers of Point Lobos and Yankee Point. Downstairs, another more casual restaurant, the California Market, also has a stunning view of the coast from tables on an open deck overlooking the swimming pool.

A few refurbished cottages near the pool are the only other remnants of the past. Most of the guest units are new suites and two-story town houses resplendent with wood-burning fireplaces, private decks, large whirlpool baths and fully equipped kitchens with an "honor bar" stocked with wine and cheese. The rooms are decorated with contemporary furnishings and Italian linen fabrics. But all have those magnificent ocean views, punctuated by graceful Monterey pines.

Although Highlands Inn is only a short drive from Carmel or Monterey, the resort was conceived as a self-contained getaway. In addition to the large kidney-shaped swimming pool, three outdoor hot tubs are scattered around the grounds. Tennis courts have recently been installed. And you can always hike or bike along trails in the hills above the inn—or walk along its private beach and muse on Robinson Jeffers' description of the Monterey coast: "The greatest meeting of land and water in the world."

HIGHLANDS INN, Highway 1 South (P.O. Box 1700), Carmel, California 93921. Telephone: (408) 624-3801, in California (800) 682-4811, nationwide (800) 538-9525. Accommodations: 146 units, mostly one- and two-bedroom suites with queen- or king-size beds; private baths with spa tubs and stall showers; some rooms fully equipped for the handicapped; telephones; television. Rates: very expensive, no meals included. Pacific's Edge restaurant open to the public for breakfast, lunch and dinner; California Market open to the public for lunch and dinner; full bar service. Children welcome. No pets. Cards: AE, CB, DC, MC, VISA. Conference facilities. Open all year.

Getting There: The inn is located on Highway 1, about four miles south of Carmel.

Turn-of-the-Century Seaside Resort
SANTA CRUZ

In 1791 the Spanish padres erected the Santa Cruz Mission at the north end of Monterey Bay. By the 1890s the town had become the queen of the seaside resorts, noted for its boardwalk, casino and fashionable homes on the hill behind the beach. In this century, however, the town's status as a resort declined; the old Victorians near the beach were turned into cheap rooming houses or replaced by boxlike motels; and the boardwalk became best known for its giant amusement park, annual Miss California pageants and shoddy clientele. Then in the 1960s the construction of a University of California campus on the hills behind the city infused a new life into Santa Cruz, including a gigantic downtown renovation. Now an effort is being made to reclaim the beach area by restoring the run-down Victorians for bed and breakfast inns.

Even if the boardwalk is too honky-tonk for your taste, there are many other beaches along the bay, plus pier-fishing facilities and deep-sea charters. Stream fishing, hiking and nature trails are found in the redwood forested Santa Cruz Mountains that rise behind the town. And just six miles north of town, a steam-powered narrow-gauge railroad provides a scenic ride through the big trees and, like the restored Victorians, is a reminder of a bygone era.

Getting There: From Monterey take Highway 1 north. From San Francisco take Highway 280 to San Jose and Highway 17 through Las Gatos to Santa Cruz.

Queen of the Boardwalk's B&Bs
CHATEAU VICTORIAN
Santa Cruz

One of the restored relics of the past, a block from the boardwalk, is Chateau Victorian. Today, with its exterior freshly painted in burnt-orange with brown trim, the elegant house seems out of place among the nondescript hotels around it. But once inside, you are treated to every luxury a country inn can offer. Owner/innkeepers Franz and Alice-June Benjamin spent over a year on the renovation, adding modern tiled baths and plush burgundy carpeting throughout. Five of the seven bedrooms have wood-burning fireplaces, some with marble facades. One room has a marvelous canopied four-poster, while brass or iron bedsteads are used in other rooms. Springlike Laura Ashley prints adorn the walls, bedding, curtains and shades and the rooms are appointed with comfortable wing or lounge chairs, plants and flowers. One of these rooms opens to a flower-filled brick patio in the rear, which separates the main house from a small building with two other units.

Franz Benjamin, a former engineer from Menlo Park, loves his new profession and his adopted city. He takes pride in serving products of the area, such as croissants and bagels from nearby bakeries and fresh fruits from local orchards. Breakfast is served at little tables covered with burgundy-and-white striped cloths in the dining area or, on balmy days, out on a secluded deck. Over coffee, let Benjamin help you with your plans for the day. He is a good guide to the area.

CHATEAU VICTORIAN, 118 First Street, Santa Cruz, California 95060. Telephone: (408) 458-9458. Accommodations: seven rooms with queen-size beds; private baths with tub/shower or shower; no telephones; no television. Rates, moderate to expensive, Continental breakfast included. No children. No pets. No smoking. Cards: AE, MC, VISA. Open all year.

Getting There: From Highway 1 take Ocean into Santa Cruz. Turn right on Barson and left on Campbell, which becomes Riverside after it crosses the river. Turn right on Second, left on Cliff and right on First.

A Creek That Tells Many a Tale

THE BABBLING BROOK INN

Santa Cruz

Long before the Spaniards settled Santa Cruz, this brook that babbles through the hills above the town was offering hospitality of sorts. The Ohlone Indians lived on the wooded cliffs above this creek, where they fished and bathed. In 1796 the mission fathers built a gristmill on the stream, which was later the site of a tannery. Early in this century, a dozen silent movies were filmed by the side of the brook in a log cabin that is now the nucleus of the present three-story house. Early residents included a vice-consul of the last Russian czar and, later, a European countess (allegedly self-proclaimed). Both entertained lavishly. Then for some forty years the building housed the Babbling Brook restaurant and finally, in 1981, became Santa Cruz's first B&B.

Surrounded by redwoods, the main house, with its wide deck overlooking a waterfall and the creek, holds the common room, where comfortable chairs and sofas cluster around a big fireplace. Wine and cheese are offered here in the evening, and breakfast is served at round tables for two. Usually a hot dish is provided, with homemade muffins and breads, orange juice and a platter of three or four fruits.

Four of the bedrooms also occupy the old house, while another eight are located next door in a recently built pair of shingled two-story

units. The beds are picture-pretty, with eyelet or floral print comforters, dust ruffles and a plethora of pillows. All but two of the rooms have mini-Franklin-type fireplaces, and most have private decks overlooking the brook or the lovely garden, which extends up a steep hillside to a stone wall built by the Ohlone Indians. Below are a stone patio and a barbecue pit (built by the countess when she occupied the place), an old wishing well and a brand-new gazebo with a hot tub.

Tom and Helen King, the present owner-innkeepers, are no strangers to the hospitality business. He started Braniff's hotel division and developed hotels throughout the world. Innkeeping also comes naturally to Helen. After raising six children and caring for a houseful of their friends, she says, "I'm just doing what I always did, except on a grander scale."

THE BABBLING BROOK INN, 1025 Laurel Street, Santa Cruz, California 95060. Telephone: (408) 427-2437. Accommodations: twelve rooms with queen- and king-size beds; private baths with tub/shower in most; wheelchair access; telephones; television. Rates: moderate to expensive, breakfast included. Children over 12 welcome. No pets. Smoking discouraged in guest rooms. Cards: AE, MC, VISA. Open all year.

Getting There: From Highway 1, turn left on Laurel Street in Santa Cruz.

SAN FRANCISCO BAY AREA

San Francisco
The Peninsula, Marin County
Berkeley and Benicia

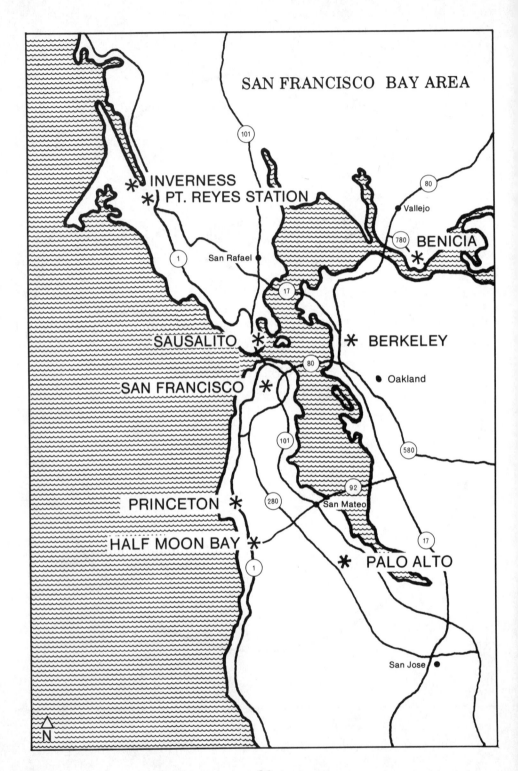

SAN FRANCISCO BAY AREA

101

80

Vallejo

INVERNESS

PT. REYES STATION

780

BENICIA

1

San Rafael

17

SAUSALITO

BERKELEY

80

Oakland

SAN FRANCISCO

101

580

PRINCETON

280

92

San Mateo

HALF MOON BAY

17

1

PALO ALTO

San Jose

N

A Conglomerate of Colorful Neighborhoods
SAN FRANCISCO

San Francisco is the needle's eye through which the threads of California history have converged. Spanish missionaries first brought Western culture here in 1776. But it was the fortunes in gold from the Mother Lode in the 1850s and later the silver from the Comstock that built the magnificent city by the Golden Gate. To her teeming port came the European immigrants who planted California's fertile valleys with grapes and returned their wines to San Francisco's splendid tables. And from the redwood forests to the north came the lumber for the houses that soon covered her hills and valleys. The fire of 1906 obliterated most of the Victorian houses east of Van Ness Avenue, but many thousands of Victorians still impart a nineteenth-century aura to the outlying neighborhoods. A 1976 survey of only nine districts—not even including the well-preserved Pacific Heights and Cow Hollow—catalogued over thirteen thousand extant Victorian structures.

Today San Francisco is a city of intimate neighborhoods and each has a distinctive character that is usually missed by visitors who stay at the downtown hotels. But now a number of small hostelries have opened in the neighborhoods, many in Victorians. These offer the charm and hospitality of a country inn, while being only ten or fifteen minutes from the heart of town.

Getting There: The quickest routes to the inns of San Francisco will vary depending on what part of the city you are coming from. If you're not familiar with the city, your first purchase should be a street map. For the sake of simplicity here, directions to each inn are given from Van Ness Avenue. If you are entering the city from the east or south, follow the freeway signs to the Golden Gate Bridge until you come to the Van Ness exit. If you are entering via the Golden Gate Bridge, follow the signs to downtown and Lombard. Go east on Lombard to Van Ness and turn right.

Grand Hotel on an Intimate Scale

THE SHERMAN HOUSE

San Francisco

This extraordinary hostelry is in a class by itself, and class it does have. The magnificent Pacific Heights mansion, with only fourteen rooms or suites, is closer to the size of a bed and breakfast inn. But it operates in the style of a grand hotel. The house was once the home of Leland Sherman, who started his career in San Francisco sweeping streets but in his twenties became the owner of the city's major music store, later known as Sherman-Clay.

Sherman moved into this exquisite Italianate-baroque villa in 1876 and several decades later built an adjoining three-story colonnaded music salon, where he entertained the prominent musicians of the day; very often, they entertained his other guests. Caruso sang here regularly, and the grand piano was played by Paderewski. Victor Herbert, Lillian Russell, Lotta Crabtree and Lola Montez were among other distinguished visitors to the Sherman House.

In the early 1980s Manouchehr Mobedshahi, an Iranian-born San Francisco economist, bought and restored the mansion, along with a rear carriage house and the formal English gardens, which Thomas Church had originally designed. The interiors were created by the late Billy Gaylord—one of the last projects of this noted designer. Most of the suites are done in the style of the Second Empire, and some are in Biedermeier, with authentic furnishings that Gaylord tracked down at auctions all over the world. "I sought the effect of an elegant French private home," he said, "such as that of the home of the Baron Rothschild in Paris."

Carrara marble fireplaces were installed in the guest rooms, where the beds have feather mattresses, down quilts and brocade canopies. In many rooms you can enjoy spectacular views of the bay from window seats that are extravagantly strewn with a dozen or more down pillows. In most rooms the walls are not papered but upholstered with padded fabric. Even the paint jobs are a work of art. In the Biedermeier suites, for example, the wainscoting and cornice are hand painted in the *faux bois* technique to emulate natural wood. The bathrooms have walls and fixtures of South American black granite and tiny TV sets so you don't miss the morning news.

The Sherman Suite is the place to stay if you plan to entertain here. It opens to a private cobblestone terrace, big enough to gracefully accommodate thirty people, with a panoramic view of the bay from the

The Sherman House

Golden Gate to Russian Hill. The large executive suites in the carriage house lend themselves to parties, too—particularly the lower unit, which has its own private terrace, garden and gazebo.

For even more grandiose entertaining, guests may take over the impressive music hall, which of course has a Sherman-Clay grand piano. But not to worry if you have no pianist; classical music is piped through the house, and in the music room it's accompanied by the soft serenade of a colony of finches who inhabit a bird cage built to look like a French château. Up a grand staircase is a more intimate salon with couches and chairs arranged for conversation groups, a fireplace and a bar.

Sherman House employs a Swiss chef who, with the help of two sous-chefs, turns out elegant breakfasts, lunches and dinners for hotel guests and their guests only. The public is not welcome in the dining room or the adjoining solarium and deck, where meals are also served, on Royal Dalton china. Breakfast is anything you want, while for dinner the chef prepares an eight- or nine-course *menu dégustation*. There is twenty-four-hour room service, too. As in most grand hotels, meals are not included in the room rate, but if you have to ask, you shouldn't come here.

If you arrive in San Francisco by air, a chauffeured vintage limousine from the Sherman House will meet your plane. During your stay here, the concierge will arrange just about anything you need, from word-processing services to personalized shopping, from translation of foreign documents to temporary privileges in local clubs. Want to charter a yacht? That's no problem either.

THE SHERMAN HOUSE, 2160 Green Street, San Francisco, California 94123. Telephone: (415) 563-3600. Accommodations: fourteen rooms and suites with twin or queen-size beds; private baths with tub/shower, some with Jacuzzi; telephones; remote-control color television. Rates: very expensive, no meals included. Children welcome. No pets. Cards: AE, MC, VISA. Facilities for weddings and small conferences. Open all year.

Getting There: From Van Ness Avenue, turn west on Green. From the Golden Gate Bridge, take Lombard to Filbert and turn right. Turn left on Green. The hotel has valet parking.

Historic Pacific Heights Victorian
HERMITAGE HOUSE
San Francisco

This seventeen-room, four-story Greek Revival mansion is sited a block away from Pacific heights's Lafayette Park in an area studded with Victorians. The house was built at the turn of the century for Judge Charles Slack and was maintained as a single-family residence until the 1970s, when it served as a drug rehabilitation center. In 1978 Ted and Marian Binkley bought the place for an inn.

The carved detailing in the redwood beams, pillars and stairway scrolls of the entrance hall is exceptionally fine, as are the carved mantel and the inlaid floors of the large living room with its graceful curved bay. Marian has decorated a cozy breakfast room with mauve-and-white chintz wallpaper and matching cloths on little round tables. Magnificent leaded-glass cabinets line the walls of this room and the adjoining formal dining room, where a buffet of juices, fruits, freshly baked breads and cold cereals is laid out each morning.

Most of the bedrooms have working fireplaces, and wherever possible, sitting areas and desks are provided. The bedrooms are cheerfully papered with chintz or floral patterns; beds are brass or four-postered or canopied, and each is stacked with as many as a dozen pillows of various patterns, sizes and shapes. Comfort is the byword here. The most unusual room is Judge Slack's former study, under the

eaves on the top floor. Paneled in redwood with a gabled ceiling, the room is lined with bookshelves and has a large stone fireplace. A desk has been placed in a dormered window with a southern view of the city towards Twin Peaks.

With private-line telephones and direct bus service to Nob Hill and downtown San Francisco, Hermitage House is an ideal headquarters for people on the go. But it's also a place to relax. An upstairs refrigerator is filled with ice and cold drinks to take onto a little sundeck. Or you may laze in a chaise in the sunny western garden.

HERMITAGE HOUSE, 2224 Sacramento Street, San Francisco, California 94115. Telephone: (415) 921-5515. Accommodations: five rooms with twin, double, queen- or king-size beds, studio couches in some rooms as well; private baths with tub or shower; private-line telephones on request; television on request. Rates: moderate to expensive, breakfast included. Children discouraged. No pets. Cards: MC, VISA. Open all year.

Getting There: From Van Ness Avenue, head west on Sacramento.

Stately Mansion in Pacific Heights
JACKSON COURT
San Francisco

Jackson Court is located in a lovely old mansion that was refurbished by interior designer Suzanne Brangham in 1978. You enter the inn through a plant-filled courtyard shared by an adjacent twin house. In the gracious living room with dark ceiling beams and wooden wainscoting, a fire bids welcome under a monumental mantelpiece of carved Italian marble flanked by cinnamon velvet love seats.

The hospitable feeling is emphasized by a "welcome home" sign on the wall of the staircase that leads to the upstairs bedrooms. These are light and spacious, painted in bright colors with contrasting trims and furnished with a blend of antiques and contemporary pieces, Oriental rugs on the hardwood floors, custom-made quilts on the beds. Several of the rooms have fireplaces, and all have comfortable sitting areas, desks, color cable television and telephones with private lines. They were designed with business travelers in mind. Plants, flowers and books are scattered about.

Each of Jackson Court's three floors has a kitchen; one has a little brick fireplace. Juices, coffee or tea, croissants, muffins and jams are set out here each morning, and if you wish to cook yourself something more substantial, you are free to do so if you provide the groceries. A concierge will be happy to make your restaurant reservations as well as obtain your theater tickets and arrange your transportation.

JACKSON COURT, 2198 Jackson Street, San Francisco, California 94115. Telephone: (415) 929-7670. Accommodations: ten rooms with double, queen- and king-size beds; private baths with showers; private-line telephones; color cable television. Rates: expensive to very expensive, Continental breakfast included. Children sometimes accepted. No pets. Cards: AE, MC, VISA. Facilities for small conferences. Open all year.

Getting There: From Van Ness Avenue, head west on Jackson.

A Touch of England off Union Street
THE BED & BREAKFAST INN
San Francisco

San Francisco's first urban inn occupies two brightly painted Italianate houses in a cul-de-sac off Union Street. Long before the bed and breakfast craze swept America, Marily and Robert Kavanaugh dreamed of opening a guest house patterned after England's B&Bs. Finally in 1976 they found the perfect building, a former boardinghouse, remodeled it with extraordinary flair, and decorated it with family heirlooms from England, combined with vividly colored contemporary accents. Two years later they purchased the house next door and added three other units.

The Bed and Breakfast Inn is a place for romance, and its *pièce de résistance* is a room in the second house called Celebration. Here a queen-size bed reposes in an alcove papered and curtained with a dainty blue and white Laura Ashley print. A love seat upholstered in blue velvet occupies a little sitting area. And beyond a divider containing pots of blooming flowers is a sunken double bathtub surrounded by brown-tinted mirrors. Downstairs is a suite named Mandalay that is decorated with grass cloth, rattan furniture, a Burmese-style ceiling fan, and sheer draperies emulating mosquito netting around the queen-size bed. On awakening, one would expect to see the dawn come up "like thunder outer China 'crost the Bay."

93

Next door the Victorian first restored by the Kavanaughs houses the breakfast area, a library and four bedrooms, each with a distinctive name and color theme inspired by boldly patterned quilts. Green Park and Kensington Garden open to a flower-filled deck behind the inn. A fifth unit on the top floor was formerly the Kavanaughs' living quarters. This penthouse suite has a living room, a dining area, a full kitchen and a latticed terrace filled with plants. A spiral staircase leads up to a bedroom loft that, like Celebration, is outfitted with a double bathtub.

In the sitting/breakfast room, a Windsor table is set with Copeland china that belonged to Marily's grandmother, and English country prints are on the wall. Downstairs the cozy library contains a game table for backgammon, cards or puzzles, a color television and a leather-bound collection of the works of Dickens.

All the rooms show Marily's gracious touches. A bouquet of fresh spring flowers on the nightstand. A bowl of fruit and selection of current magazines on a table. Beds turned down to reveal the pretty printed sheets and pillowcases. And on each pillow—a fortune cookie.

Breakfast is as important as the beds here. Marily serves juice, freshly ground coffee, hot croissants or occasionally "sticky buns" on her antique flowered chinaware. Some guests prefer to be served in the breakfast room or outdoors on umbrella-covered tables in the flower-filled garden. But Marily prefers to pamper you with a breakfast tray in bed.

The Bed and Breakfast inn is located in San Francisco's Cow Hollow district, named for the dairy farms that once covered the area. The neighborhood is a treasure trove of Victorian architecture, notably along Union Street, where the colorfully painted old houses have been turned into fashionable shops, bars and restaurants. A bus line leads directly to downtown San Francisco.

THE BED AND BREAKFAST INN, 4 Charlton Court (off Union between Buchanan and Laguna), San Francisco, California 94123. Telephone: (415) 921-9784. Accommodations: ten rooms with twin, double, queen- or king-size beds; shared half-baths with tub/shower or shower only; private baths with shower or double tub; telephones and television in suites. Rates: moderate to very expensive, Continental breakfast included. Children discouraged. Pets discouraged. Smoking permitted in public rooms only. No credit cards. Open all year.

Getting There: From Van Ness, turn west on Union to Charlton Court and turn left.

The Bed and Breakfast Inn

WASHINGTON SQUARE INN
San Francisco

While the affluent citizens of San Francisco were building their palatial residences on Nob Hill and Pacific Heights, the working-class immigrants settled in North Beach. The city's ethnic mix is particularly mirrored in Washington Square, a small park at the base of Telegraph Hill. This square started out ignobly in the 1840s as the potato patch of Juana Briones, the Hill's first settler, and was later dubbed the Spanish Lot. In 1849 the area around the park became known as Little Chile, when the gold rush lured an influx of Chilean settlers here. Later came the Italians, who moored their fishing boats at the nearby wharves, and then the Chinese, whose homes and shops have spread into North Beach from neighboring Chinatown.

Today in the early mornings office workers walk their dogs in Washington Square, while runners jog and middle-aged Chinese faithfully perform their graceful t'ai chi exercises. Later in the day, elderly Italian gentlemen take over the park benches, reading *Italo-Americana*. On the square's western perimeter, once the site of a Russian Orthodox church, the Washington Square Bar & Grill attracts a sophisticated mix of literary types. Chimes peal across the park from the imposing tower of Saints Peter and Paul Catholic Church on the square's northern boundary. And on the east side, with a view of the park and Russian Hill beyond, is the Washington Square Inn.

In 1978 this two-story corner building was totally refurbished by interior designer Nan Rosenblatt, who has subsequently opened the Inn at Union Square and the Garden Court Hotel in Palo Alto. In the lobby, a Continental breakfast of freshly squeezed orange juice, croissants and scones is served beside an intricately carved fireplace. In the late afternoon, tea is offered, with cucumber sandwiches and shortbread cookies. Guests may also purchase a bottle of wine from the inn's cellar of California varietals and champagnes.

The inn's fifteen bedrooms are individually decorated with bright French florals and chinoiserie; each is coordinated around a different color. Antique armoires, dressers and tables are scattered about; most of the beds are draped with colorful canopies. Three of the rooms are large bedroom-sitting room combinations with sofa beds that make them suitable for families of four. The others vary from spacious to small. The front rooms overlooking the square are, of course, the best.

Here, from a seat by the bay window, you may observe the colorful goings-on in the park.

Washington Square is midway between downtown San Francisco and Fisherman's Wharf—a short bus ride or a ten-minute walk from each. There is, however, much to see and do in the immediate vicinity. A block away is upper Grant Avenue—the center of the Beat movement of the 1950s and now the site of a conglomeration of crafts shops, antique stores, coffeehouses and so forth; a few blocks south, Grant leads into Chinatown. Strollers will delight in exploring the picturesque lanes hidden behind the main streets of Telegraph and Russian hills. If you wish to wander farther afield, the inn's manager will arrange a car rental or just about anything else to enhance your visit—theater tickets, a tour, a stenographer or a picnic.

WASHINGTON SQUARE INN, 1660 Stockton Street, San Francisco, California 94133. Telephone: (415) 981-4220. Accommodations: fifteen rooms with twin, double, queen- or king-size beds; private and shared baths with tub or shower or tub/shower; telephones; televisions on request. Rates: moderate to very expensive, Continental breakfast included. Children welcome. No pets. Cards: AE, MC, VISA. Open all year.

Getting There: From Van Ness Avenue take Union Street east to Stockton and turn left.

In the Style of the 1890s
VICTORIAN INN ON THE PARK
San Francisco

In the 1890s many wealthy San Franciscans built their mansions along the Panhandle, a wooded, grassy plot one block wide and eight blocks long leading to Golden Gate Park. One of these houses—an ornate four-story Victorian with an open Belvedere tower—was built in 1897 for Thomas Clunie, a prominent lawyer and United States congressman. In more recent years the house was occupied by a cult group that believed in rebirthing, a rite that took place in a hot tub in the basement. Now the house itself has been reborn under the aegis of Lisa and William Benau, who have faithfully restored its turn-of-the-century splendor for an inn.

The parquet floors are inlaid with oak, mahogany and redwood, the entry hall is intricately paneled in mahogany and the dining room has

97

oak wainscotings with an unusual spooled plate rack. The Benaus furnished the inn with authentic period pieces: velvet-upholstered Queen Anne chair and sofa in the parlor, brass and carved wood headboards in the bedrooms, marble-topped sinks in the baths. Six guest rooms occupy the second floor. The largest has a fireplace and view of the Panhandle from the curved bay of the tower. The smallest is a light-splashed glassed-in porch with a sunken tub in the bath. And the most unusual is decorated in art deco style with accents of stained glass and posters. Four other rooms share the top floor, one of which claims the open tower as its private deck.

Breakfast, served in the dining room, consists of fresh fruit, orange juice, flaky croissants and homemade breads. If guests wish, the Benaus will arrange catered dinners or allow the use of a small library for private meetings, which makes the inn attractive for business travelers.

With the Panhandle parkway at its front door, this inn is also popular with walkers and joggers. Golden Gate Park, the largest man-made park in the world, is only seven blocks away. At its entrance bicycles can be rented for exploring one-thousand acres of flower-filled meadows, woods, streams and lakes. The park is also the site of the de Young and Asian Art museums, the California Academy of Sciences and the Japanese Tea Garden.

VICTORIAN INN ON THE PARK, 301 Lyon Street, San Francisco, California 94117. Telephone: (415) 931-1830. Accommodations: twelve rooms with twin or queen-size beds; private baths with tub/shower or stall shower; telephones and television upon request. Rates: expensive, Continental breakfast included. Small children discouraged. No pets. Smoking discouraged. Cards: AE, MC, VISA. Open all year.

Getting There: From Van Ness Avenue, take Fell Street west to Lyon. The inn is on the corner.

Victorian Inn on the Park

Turn-of-the-Century Haight Ashbury Showplace
THE SPRECKELS MANSION
San Francisco

The Haight Ashbury district has become again a quiet residential neighborhood after enduring a turbulent notoriety in the 1960s as the blossoming place for San Francisco's flower children. This area on the northern slopes of Twin Peaks was countryside until the 1890s, when a flurry of building activity made it a popular suburb. Today some twelve hundred relics of Victorian architecture line its streets. One of these houses, a splendid example of the Colonial Revival style, was built in 1898 for Richard Spreckels, superintendent of the Western Sugar Refinery owned by his uncle, sugar baron Claus Spreckels.

The stately mansion, facing the heavily wooded Buena Vista Park, was well maintained as a single-family residence until 1979 when Jeffrey Ross and Johathan Shannon turned it into a spectacular inn. "The house has had a way of adapting to the times and attracting artistic people," Ross observes. Ambrose Bierce and Jack London supposedly worked in the top-floor ballroom at one time. And during the 1960s the producer for the Grateful Dead rock band owned the house and used the old ballroom as a recording studio.

When Ross and Shannon bought the house, an amazing amount of its original embellishments were still intact: seven fireplaces, some with rare detailing such as a tortoiseshell tile hearth in the master bedroom; hand-painted Meissen chandeliers; museum-quality windows of leaded stained glass, many with art nouveau overtones; embossed wall

coverings with gilt friezes; Corinthian columns in the hall and parlor. Ross and Shannon blended French and English turn-of-the-century antiques with pieces from other periods, including contemporary furnishings. All of the rooms have sitting areas with wing chairs, and throughout are fanciful touches. The bed in one room, for example, is set in a columned alcove with a canopy swooping up to Corinthian capitals. Many of the bedrooms—and even the master bathroom—have fireplaces, and most have views of Buena Vista Park or look out over Golden Gate Park to the ocean.

The third-floor ballroom is now a stunning two-bedroom suite, decorated with contemporary furniture and Oriental accessories. A gabled redwood ceiling rises some thirty feet over the living room, where sofas covered with navy-blue suede flank the large fireplace. Raised sitting areas in two large dormers command spectacular views of the city. Golden Gate Park, the ocean and the Marin headlands.

Next door to the mansion is a handsome Edwardian building that was built as a guest house around 1900 and is now part of the inn. The bedrooms are designed to inspire fantasies. Entering the very Edwardian English Rose, one would not be surprised to find Sherlock Holmes sitting in the black wing chair in front of the brick fireplace. In Sunset Suite, where a view of the ocean is framed by stained-glass panels, the decor is reminiscent of a room in the French countryside. Gypsy Hideaway has a view and a fireplace, and a paisley-engulfed bed that will make you think you've been abducted by a gypsy caravan. And the many skylights in Stargazers' Suite encourage flights of fancy to outer space; this suite also has a magnificent western view and an unusual fireplace.

In the mornings trays of juice, croissants and coffee are brought to the rooms at Spreckels Mansion. In the evenings refreshments are served in the library of the main house. From here it's a pleasant stroll past rows of colorful Victorians to Haight Street, where the former hippie hangouts have been transformed into nice shops and restaurants.

THE SPRECKELS MANSION, 737 Buena Vista West, San Francisco 94117. Telephone: (415) 861-3008. Accommodations: ten rooms with queen-size beds; some shared baths, mostly private baths with tub and/or shower; telephones; television on request. Rates: expensive to very expensive, Continental breakfast included. Children sometimes accepted. No pets. Cards: AE, MC, VISA. Open all year.

Getting There: From Van Ness go west on market to Haight and head west to Buena Vista West.

French Château on Alamo Square
THE ARCHBISHOP'S MANSION
San Francisco

In 1851 the City of San Francisco annexed the farmlands west of Van Ness Avenue between the Haight-Ashbury hills and Pacific Heights. This area, known as the Western Addition, was a popular suburb in the 1880s and 1890s and, as it was spared from the great fire of 1906, it still contains hundreds of Victorian houses. Some of the most beautiful examples of these picturesque buildings face Alamo Square, a small park on a sloping hillside. On its north side stands a stately three-story mansion with a slate mansard roof that looks like a manor house in the French countryside. It was built in 1904 as a residence for Archbishop Patrick Riordan and for four decades he and his successors entertained Catholic dignitaries from all over the world in the imposing first-floor reception rooms. Pope Pius XII stayed here in the mid-1930s when he was still a cardinal.

In recent decades the Alamo Square district sharply declined. The archbishop's home became a boys' school and in the 1970s was used as a half-way house by a local hospital. But the area was recently designated as a historic preservation district and the fine old buildings around the square are mostly restored. Some now hold inns, of which the most spectacular is the Archbishop's Manion, another exquisite creation of Jonathan Shannon and Jeffrey Ross, owners of the Spreckels Mansion.

In the grand hall a splendid brass chandelier from France hangs from the coffered mahogany ceiling. Fourteen-foot-high redwood columns with intricately carved capitals flank the base of a three-story stairway crowned with an oval dome of stained glass. In the formal parlor, the triple-vaulted ceiling is painted with a motif derived from a Louis XIV carpet, an embellishment added by Shannon and Ross. Wood-burning fireplaces, most with mirrored and carved mantels, enhance almost every room of the house, including all but two of the fifteen guest units.

Shannon and Ross resisted the temptation to use a clerical theme in decorating the Archbishop's Mansion. Instead they named the rooms and suites after romantic nineteenth-century operas, since the San Francisco Opera House is only six blocks away. They also nixed Victorian decor, opting for museum-quality French furnishings that reflect the Second Empire style of the house. One of the most impressive pieces came from a castle in the south of France—a massive

102

The Archbishop's Mansion

four-poster bed with cherubs carved on its walnut canopy and headboard. "If that doesn't get you to heaven, nothing will," Ross quips. A bedstead with ivory inlays of Japanese ladies sets the theme for Madame Butterfly's room. A chaise upholstered in silver velvet reclines on a base of gilded silver swans in Der Rosenkavalier's enormous bath-sitting room. And there's also a chaise—plus a fireplace and freestanding tub—in Carmen's bathroom. In the third-floor rooms the mansard dormers are fitted with window seats for a peek at the square or the city's hills and skyscrapers rising above the neighboring rooftops. The archbishop's chapel, which was also located on this floor, now serves as a spacious meeting room.

Shannon and Ross are making a strong bid for the conference business and for weddings and receptions, which may be held in the gracious lower rooms. But to make sure that the inn's guests are not disturbed by these goings-on, a large sitting room on the second floor, facing the square, has been allocated for their exclusive use.

A Continental buffet breakfast is served in the enormous dining room, which is papered in silk patterned with ivory fleur-de-lis. This room, which can seat sixty-five, and a smaller dining room, which seats twelve, may be used for catered dinners by guests at the Archbishop's Mansion and at the other inns surrounding Alamo Square—recalling an early tradition of this house, when His Excellency offered hospitality after the 1906 fire to the homeless San Franciscans who camped in the square.

THE ARCHBISHOP'S MANSION, 100 Fulton Street, San Francisco, 94117. Telephone: (415) 563-7872. Accommodations: fifteen rooms with queen- or two queen-size beds; private baths with tubs and showers or stall showers; direct-dial telephones; television available on request. Rates: expensive to very expensive, Continental breakfast included. Children discouraged. No pets. No smoking in most public rooms. Cards: AE, MC, VISA. Facilities for conferences and weddings. Open all year.

Getting There: From Van Ness Avenue head west on Fell to Steiner and turn right to Fulton; the inn is on the corner. Offstreet parking for eight cars; nearby church lots available for valet parking during receptions.

THE WILLOWS INN
San Francisco

Window boxes filled with geraniums distinguish this three-story building from its look-alike neighbors near the bustling intersection of Church and upper Market streets. The inn occupies the top two floors above a French restaurant, but at the top of the stairs, a stand of pussy willows in the reception area ushers you into a peaceful world.

The Willows derives its name from the unusual furniture of bent willow wood made especially for the inn and found throughout in the form of headboards, sofas, chaises and chairs. The graceful willoware gives a countryish look to this hostelry near the heart of the city, as do the Laura Ashley prints that bloom in pastel shades of lilac, blue, peach and green on the walls, bedspreads and ruffled pillows of every room. Wooden shutters, bouquets of dried and fresh flowers, and serigraphs by Graciela Boulanger complete the setting. There are no private baths, but each room is outfitted with a washbasin and a terrycloth bathrobe for the trip down the hall.

Beverages are offered each evening in the small parlor. You may have your morning orange juice, coffee and croissants here, but most guests prefer service in their rooms. The pretty tray is done in pink and comes with a carnation and the morning paper. At night a turned-down bed and a mint greet you.

Proprietors Rachmael ben Avram and Gerard Lespinette cater to the business traveler. The Muni underground streetcar stops at the inn's front door and will whisk you downtown in minutes. The innkeepers will line up car rentals, restaurant reservations, secretarial and duplicating services, and almost anything else you might require. It's like having an office staff away from home. Many business travelers will also find they have a lot in common with their genial hosts, for French-born Gerard was a banker in Paris before coming to this country in the late 1970s and innkeeping is Rachmael's third career. He formerly was active in the theater as a stage and company director and most recently served as the national director of the Gucci stores. Their lives changed, however, several years ago when a friend casually commented: "You like to entertain so much, I see you as innkeepers." They agreed and they love it.

THE WILLOWS INN, 710 Fourteenth Street, San Francisco, California 94114. Telephone: (415) 431-4770. Accommodations: eleven rooms with double or queen-size beds; four shared shower rooms, some with tub/shower, and four shared lavatories; direct-dial telephones; no television. Rates: moderate, Continental breakfast included. Children over eight welcome. No pets. Cards: AE, MC, VISA. Open all year.

Getting There: From Van Ness Avenue take Market Street west to the intersection of Church and Fourteenth; turn right on Fourteenth. Off-street parking provided for a nominal charge.

Italianate Mansion in the Sunny Mission

THE INN SAN FRANCISCO
San Francisco

In 1776 the Spanish chose the flattest and warmest part of San Francisco as a site for Mission Dolores and its surrounding farmlands. The area was ignored by later settlers until the 1860s, when a streetcar line connected the boom town of San Francisco with the sunny fields to the south, and amusement parks, a racetrack and fashionable homes lured gold-rich San Franciscans to the Mission. In this century, however, the affluent moved to the hills of the north and abandoned the area "South of the Slot" to working-class residents and a growing number of Latin American immigrants. But the pendulum again swung to the Mission in the 1960s, when a new generation of San Franciscans discovered the bargain-priced Victorians there and the blue skies that bless the district when most of the city is shrouded by fog.

Among the newcomers was Joel Daily, who restored an 1872 three-story Italianate mansion that had been converted into a hotel. The inn opened in 1980, but the improvements never end. Downstairs, the double parlor with its fourteen-foot ceilings is resplendent with redwood paneling and wainscoting and carved fireplaces. Here inn guests are treated to a morning buffet of pastries, hard-cooked eggs and tropical fruits.

Most of the inn's fifteen bedrooms have private baths, a few have hot-tubs-for-two with views, and a first-floor room has its own private outdoor spa. These pools, however, are somewhat redundant, because Joel has just built a lovely large spa house for use by all the guests in a side garden. Another favorite place to relax here is a roof deck that commands a panoramic view of San Francisco and the mountains of Marin beyond.

The Inn San Francisco

Despite all the renovation that is going on, the Mission District today is still a mixed neighborhood, economically and ethnically. The brightly painted restored Victorians along South Van Ness are interspersed with run-down buildings and commercial properties, and a block away on Mission Street you are likely to hear more Spanish than English. The area is only minutes from downtown by bus or BART, and it has the best weather in the city.

THE INN SAN FRANCISCO, 943 South Van Ness Avenue, San Francisco, California 94110. Telephone: (415) 641-0188. Accommodations: fifteen rooms with double, queen-size or two queen-size beds, rollaways available; most rooms have private baths with tub/shower, tub or stall shower; direct-dial telephones; color television. Rates: moderate to expensive, breakfast included. Children over 14 welcome. No pets. Cards: AE, MC, VISA. Open all year.

Getting There: Take Van Ness Avenue south across Market, where it becomes South Van Ness. Parking garage across the street from inn.

Luxurious Haven Near the Theaters and Shops
THE INN AT UNION SQUARE
San Francisco

For those who want to stay in the heart of San Francisco, the Inn at Union Square offers a personalized alternative to the commercial hotels. One-half block from the square and its elegant shops, the inn had been a sixty-room transient hotel, vacant for some years, when it was renovated in 1980 by interior designer Nan Rosenblatt, owner of the Washington Square Inn. She cut the number of guest units to thirty, creating some two-room suites from the smaller rooms and a luxurious sixth-floor suite with a fireplace, wet bar, whirlpool bath and sauna.

The decor and service at the Inn at Union Square are very similar to those of the Inn at Washington Square. The bedrooms are furnished with English antiques; bright fabrics drape the beds and cover the goose-down pillows. Fresh flowers are set in the rooms. Each floor has a little lobby with a fireplace, where an English tea is served in the afternoons, along with hors d'oeuvres. Bottles of wine may be purchased from the inn. A Continental breakfast—croissants, juice, fruit and coffee—is served by this fireside or in the rooms.

108

Also, as at Washington Square, the Inn at Union Square has a concierge to take care of restaurant reservations, theater tickets and the like. Valet parking is available at the door.

THE INN AT UNION SQUARE, 440 Post Street, San Francisco, California 94102. Telephone (415) 397-3510. Accommodations: thirty rooms with twin, queen- or king-size beds; private baths with tub/shower; telephones; color television. Rates: expensive to very expensive, Continental breakfast included. Children welcome. No pets. Cards: AE, MC, VISA. Open all year.

Getting There: From Van Ness Avenue go east on Post Street.

European Country Ambience in the Center of Town
PETITE AUBERGE
WHITE SWAN INN
San Francisco

Halfway up Nob Hill from Union Square, these small sister hotels offer the charm of a French or English country inn and every personalized service you can imagine. An attendant will park your car and a houseman will escort you to your room, where the scent of potpourri fills the air and a flick of a switch starts a gas flame in the fireplace. Each room is richly appointed with countryish flowered wallpaper, antique writing desks, comfortable chairs or sofas, plants, bowls of fresh fruit and armoires that conceal color television sets.

Although the amenities are the same at both hotels, their decors are different. Petite Auberge is frilly French with its baroque facade, ruffled muslin curtains and quilted spreads. The newer White Swan is done up in a cooler English style, with white shuttered windows, white spreads, Laura Ashley prints and tones of aquamarine, mauve and burgundy throughout. Both are older hotels that have been renovated by Roger and Sally Post, who also own the Gosby House and Green Gables Inn in Pacific Grove.

Petite Auberge and White Swan both have lovely parlors, with fireplaces, where afternoon tea is served; the White Swan also has a handsome very British library with another fireplace and a fine selection of books. Adjacent to the parlor in each inn is a breakfast room, where a substantial morning buffet is offered—fruit juices, breads, pastries, muffins, cereals, granola, cheese and a main dish that changes daily, sometimes a soufflé or frittata or quiche. For fine weather, there are outdoor eating areas, too.

At each inn a concierge will help with your dinner reservations. When you return to your room, your bed will be turned down and a Swiss chocolate and a rose will be on the pillow. Both inns are romantic places to share with someone special. But if you happen to be traveling alone, you'll find a teddy bear on the bed to cuddle with. And if you like, you can even take your furry friend home, for a price.

PETITE AUBERGE, 863 Bush Street, San Francisco, California 94108. Telephone: (415) 928-6000. Accommodations: twenty-six rooms with queen-size beds; private baths with tub/shower or stall shower; direct-dial telephones; color television. Rates: expensive to very expensive, breakfast included. Children welcome. No pets. Cards: AE, MC, VISA. Open all year.

WHITE SWAN INN, 845 Bush Street, San Francisco, California 94108. Telephone: (415) 775-1755. Accommodations: twenty-seven rooms with queen- and king-size beds; private baths with tub/shower; wet bars; direct-dial telephones; television. Rates: expensive to very expensive, breakfast included. Children welcome. No pets. Cards: AE, MC, VISA. Facilities for small conferences. Open all year.

Getting There: From Van Ness Avenue, head east on Bush.

A Bit of Cape Cod on the Pacific
PILLAR POINT INN
Princeton by-the-Sea

This pretty harbor north of Half Moon Bay has a shady history of smuggling, gambling and prostitution. But today the tiny village is a commercial and sports fishing center and the site of several good seafood restaurants. And very recently, with the construction of Pillar Point Inn in a Cape Cod style, it's a place for an overnight getaway.

The inn is located across the street from the harbor, and all eleven guest rooms have views of the boats bobbing in the water. The rooms are look-alikes, but it's a terrific look: navy blue carpeting, raised hearth of blue and white tiles, window seats with café curtains and pillows in Laura Ashley-style blue and white prints. You sleep on a feather bed covered with sheets and down quilts in the same print and no less than six ruffled pillows. Each room has a modern refrigerator encased in a replicated old-fashioned wooden ice box.

Downstairs a parlor and breakfast room are decorated in the same theme with a see-through tiled fireplace between them. Tea is offered guests in the evening, and the morning brings a breakfast of orange-banana juice, muffins and baked eggs.

PILLAR POINT INN, 380 Capistrano Road, Princeton. Mailing address: P.O. Box 388, El Granada, California 94018. Telephone: (415) 728-7377. Accommodations: eleven rooms with queen- and king-size beds; private baths with tub/shower; one room fully equipped for the handicapped; telephones; television. Rates: moderate to expensive, breakfast included. Children over 12 welcome. No pets. Smoking and nonsmoking rooms. Cards: MC, VISA. Open all year.

Getting There: From San Francisco take Highway 1 south to Princeton. Turn right and follow Capistrano Road past Pillar Point Harbor.

A Garden Haven on the Coast

MILL ROSE INN
Half Moon Bay

The coastal town of Half Moon Bay, some thirty miles south of downtown San Francisco, is becoming an increasingly popular destination spot for Bay Area residents. The town's Main Street is lined with turn-of-the-century streetlights and buildings, while the surrounding area abounds in the cultivation of artichokes and pumpkins, which create a blaze of orange in the autumn. Beaches and the fishing village of Princeton are nearby.

On a quiet side street of Half Moon Bay, the Mill Rose Inn is tucked behind a rose-covered picket fence and an English garden bursting with petunias, daisies and bougainvillea. The main house is an old-fashioned cottage with a cozy parlor and sitting room paneled in knotty pine. Adjoining it, innkeepers Eve and Terry Baldwin have built a charming two-story inn where all the antique-filled rooms have fireplaces, private entrances, pretty modern baths and refrigerators stocked with complimentary goodies.

Downstairs a fire burns in the tile-faced hearth of a lovely breakfast room, where french doors lead to the gardens on either side. In the mornings, Eve serves a full meal here, or in your room if you choose. In addition to fruits, juices, pastries and homemade jams, she offers a hot dish, such as quiche or eggs, along with bacon or sausages.

But the pride of the inn now is a new seven-foot octagonal Jacuzzi in a large gazebo behind the house. It has a private garden too. And in your room you'll find fluffy robes for your walk to the spa.

MILL ROSE INN, 615 Mill Street, Half Moon Bay, California 94019. Telephone: (415) 729-9794. Accommodations: six rooms with double, queen- and king-size beds; private baths with tub/shower or stall shower; telephones; television. Rates: expensive to very expensive, breakfast included. Children over 12 welcome. No pets. No smoking. Cards: AE, MC, VISA. Facilities for small conferences. Open all year.

Getting There: From San Francisco take Highway 280 south to Highway 92 and head west; when you reach Half Moon Bay, turn left on Main Street, then turn right on Mill Street. From Monterey, Highway 1 to San Francisco passes through Half Moon Bay.

Mill Rose Inn

Where the Little Touches Are Very Big
GARDEN COURT HOTEL
Palo Alto

This gracious mission-style structure, with wrought-iron balconies and a central courtyard filled with flowers and fountains, conjures visions of a long and colorful history. Wrong: interior designer Nan Rosenblatt built this hotel in 1986. And if you have stayed at her hostelries in San Francisco—the Inn at Union Square and Washington Square Inn—you'll recognize some of her touches in the decor.

Most of the rooms have canopy-draped four-posters, in king and queen sizes with down comforters and pillows; some have fireplaces, whirlpool tubs and balconies or terraces overlooking the courtyard. All are decorated in restful pastel hues of green, peach and mauve, and all have a comfortable sitting area. In the luxurious tiled bathrooms, you'll find a rose on the marble counter and fluffy terry-cloth robes. Little touches are important here, such as the *Wall Street Journal* delivered to your door each morning along with the local paper—and your shoes, freshly shined.

Each of the hotel's three upper floors has a sitting room where a Continental breakfast and high tea are served to the guests. But you would be just as happy sitting in the beautiful first-floor parlor/lobby, which also has a fireplace. When you enter here from the street, you first see a giant bowl of fruit, which says something about the kind of hospitality dispensed at the Garden Court.

GARDEN COURT HOTEL, 520 Cowper Street, Palo Alto, California 94301. Telephone: (415) 322-9000, in California (800) 556-9595, nationwide (800) 824-9028. Accommodations: sixty-one rooms or suites with twin doubles, queen- or king-size beds; private baths with tub/shower; some rooms fully equipped for the handicapped; telephones; remote-control television. Rates: very expensive, Continental breakfast included. Children welcome. No pets. Cards: AE, MC, VISA. Facilities for conferences and weddings. Open all year.

Getting There: Take University Avenue exit from Highway 101 and head west to Cowper Street. Turn left.

A Cascade of Cottages above the Bay

CASA MADRONA HOTEL

Sausalito

Just across the Golden Gate Bridge from San Francisco is the colorful town of Sausalito, once a Portuguese fishing village and now a chic residential community where houses cling to the steep wooded hills that rise from the bay. On one of these hillsides overlooking the harbor a stately mansion was built in 1885 for a private residence. Over the years it has metamorphosed as a hotel, bordello, beatnik boarding house, European-style pension and finally, under the ownership of John Mays, as one of the state's most elegant inns.

After buying the property in 1978 Mays restored the rooms in the mansion, decorating them in turn-of-the-century style according to different themes—one reminiscent of a bordello, another with a nautical touch and so forth. Next, he renovated three adjoining cabins for guest rooms. Then in 1983 he took the plunge—literally—and constructed a cluster of cottages that cascade down the bank from the mansion to the street that fronts the bay. Each is different with peaked roofs, dormers, bays, gables and decks and although brand new, they look like they have been there forever. Mays commissioned sixteen interior designers and gave each a free hand to decorate one of the rooms, resulting in enormously different interiors for the cottages, with a mix of styles ranging from Oriental to Victorian to art nouveau. One room emulates a country French château, another an Italian villa, another a New England summer retreat. The most unusual might be a Parisian artist's loft with skylights and a raised platform fully equipped with an easel, canvas and paints; paintings by former inhabitants of this room are hung on the walls.

Architecturally, each unit is also unique. No two are the same size and shape and none is a box: bays protrude here and there, skylighted ceilings slope at various angles and raised platforms hold beds or sitting areas. Almost all of the rooms have working fireplaces, most have private decks or balconies and all have dazzling views of the bay. The little amenities are not forgotten here either. Refrigerators are stocked with fruit juice and mineral water, bathrooms are supplied with hand lotion and a staff member is assigned full time to keep fresh flowers in the rooms.

A buffet breakfast of juice, fruits, yogurt and croissants is served in the charming dining room of the old mansion. Copies of the *Los Angeles Times, New York Times* and the *San Francisco Chronicle* are also provided. This room, with its magnificent views of the yacht harbor and Belvedere Island, becomes a romantic restaurant for lunch or dinner, when chef Stephen Simmons prepares his creative adaptations of American fare.

Many of Casa Madrona's guests are actually visitors to San Francisco who want to get away from the city milieu. Sausalito itself offers much to do with its quaint shops, crafts galleries, coffeehouses and restaurants that line the shore. And when it's time to commute to San Francisco, there's the beauty of a thirty-minute ride by ferryboat across the bay.

CASA MADRONA, 801 Bridgeway, Sausalito, California 94965. Telephone: (415) 332-0502. Accommodations: thirty-two rooms or suites with twin, double, queen- or king-size beds, roll-away beds and Japanese futon mats available; all rooms but two have private baths with tub/shower, stall shower or tub; some rooms with wheelchair access and one fully equipped for the handicapped; telephones; color television or request. Rates: moderate to very expensive, breakfast included. Restaurant open to the public for lunch and dinner. Children welcome. No pets. Cards: AE, CB, DC, MC, VISA. Facilities for small conferences. Open all year.

Getting There: From San Francisco take Highway 101 north across the Golden Gate Bridge. Take the Alexander Avenue exit and follow into center of town, which becomes Bridgeway. Marin Airporter offers service from San Francisco International Airport to Sausalito, where the hotel will pick up guests. Daily ferryboat service from Sausalito to Fisherman's Wharf or the Ferry Building in San Francisco.

Casa Madrona

POINT REYES AREA
Point Reyes Station and Inverness

The San Andreas Fault runs down the center of Tomales Bay, a long fingerlike inlet that separates Point Reyes Peninsula from the mainland. A railroad once ran along the east shore of the bay, bearing cargoes of lumber from the northern timberlands. Today Highway 1 follows its tracks, carrying carloads of Sunday drivers to the little seafood houses around the town of Marshall to feast on the bay's gastronomic gift to California: oysters. The west side of the bay shelters the village of Inverness, a popular weekend and summer resort. Beyond this is the Point Reyes National Seashore: seventy thousand acres of coastal wilderness with magnificent hiking trails and beautiful beaches. Here a model village has been built, typical of those inhabited by the Miwok Indians, who once dwelled on these shores. And here is the harbor that supposedly sheltered Sir Francis Drake's *Golden Hinde* during his expedition to the Pacific in 1579. Point Reyes is one of the best spots for bird watching in the country; over four hundred species have been observed in the park. On weekends the park rangers conduct nature walks along the beaches and lectures in the visitors centers at Bear Valley and Drakes Beach.

Getting There: From San Francisco take Highway 101 north to the San Anselmo turn-off; continue on Sir Francis Drake Boulevard (Highway 17) through Fairfax to Point Reyes Station and Inverness.

English Gardens in the Wilderness

HOLLY TREE INN
Point Reyes Station

Located in a secluded nineteen acres of forest, this inn is named for the manicured holly trees that combine with English boxwood and lilac to form a hedge around the spacious lawn with its flower-covered stone wishing well. Owners Diane and Tom Balogh live downstairs in the two-story ranch house. Upstairs guests have their own large living room, papered in blue and white Laura Ashley prints, with comfortable overstuffed sofas and chairs upholstered in matching fabrics arranged around a brick fireplace. Another copper-hooded fireplace warms the adjoining dining room, where breakfast is served; fresh fruits and juices, poppyseed bread and farm-fresh eggs are regulars on the menu. The common rooms open to a private deck sheltered by a flowery hillside. Four bedrooms, decorated with antiques, quilted bedspreads and ruffled curtains, offer views of the woodsy surroundings.

HOLLY TREE INN, 3 Silverhills Road (P.O. Box 642), Point Reyes Station, California 94956. Telephone: (415) 663-1554. Accommodations: four rooms with double, queen- and king-size beds; private baths; no telephones; no television. Rates: moderate, breakfast included. Children welcome. No pets. Smoking not permitted in guest rooms. Cards: MC, VISA. Open all year.

Getting There: From Highway 101 take Sir Francis Drake Boulevard west to Route 1. Go north on Route 1 one block and turn left at the sign for Point Reyes National Seashore Park Headquarters. Take the third left turn after passing the entrance to the park headquarters, and look for the Holly Tree Inn sign.

Peaceful Is the Word Here
TEN INVERNESS WAY
Inverness

A tranquil, homelike setting for those who want to get away from it all is provided in this spacious redwood-shingled house, built as a residence in 1904. Writer Mary Davies opened this bed and breakfast inn in 1980. She and her husband Jim Langdon live there and operate the inn with assistance from an assortment of interesting locals. A large fir-paneled living room, furnished with antiques and an Oriental rug, is a restful spot for reading during the day, but livelier in the evening when guests gather around the big stone fireplace—especially if there's someone who wants to play the player piano. A full breakfast is served in the adjoining dining room, which is cheered by a large Danish fireplace. There's always fruit, perhaps a half grapefruit, and goodies such as blueberry or banana pancakes, or scrambled eggs with toasted homemade bread. Upstairs the four bedrooms, paneled with white carsiding, are furnished with handmade patchwork quilts and rag rugs. And there are always bowls of flowers cut from the gardens that surround the inn. It was rumored that a ghost once inhabited this house, but Mary had the local Episcopal priest bless each room with holy water when the

Ten Inverness Way

inn opened. Only good spirits live here now. As Mary says, "Peaceful is the word most often used to describe our place." Still, you'll find lots of activity a block away on Tomales Bay. Mary will give you expert advice on where to hike, bike, ride horses and swim.

TEN INVERNESS WAY, 10 Inverness Way, Inverness, California 94937. Telephone: (415) 669-1648. Accommodations: four rooms with twin, double, and queen-size beds; private baths with stall shower or tub/shower; no telephones; no television. Rates: moderate, breakfast included. Children over 12 welcome. No pets. Cards: MC, VISA. Open all year.

Getting There: From San Francisco take Highway 101 north to the Sir Francis Drake Boulevard exit and continue through Olema to Inverness. Once you are in the village, turn left at the Inverness Inn Restaurant.

Romantic, Treetop Hideaway
BLACKTHORNE INN
Inverness

Here is an inn for young-at-heart romantics. The nucleus of Blackthorne is a tiny cabin, built during the 1930s on a steep forested hillside near Inverness. Then in 1975 patent attorney Bill Wigert designed an amazing structure above it, using beams from the piers in San Francisco and gigantic doors salvaged from the Southern Pacific depot. An eight-sided tower with a spiral staircase rises from the cabin through two floors flanked with decks to an octagonal eagle's nest room, topped by a platform that peeks out of the treetops some seventy feet above the ground. Bridges connect the tower rooms to hillside walkways banked with rhododendrons and to another deck with a hot tub, cold tub and bath house.

Wigert and his wife Susan have recently enlarged the two bedrooms in the main cabin. Both have private entrances and sitting areas and one has a private deck. Above are a glass-walled solarium and the living room with its dramatic, skylighted A-frame ceiling of rough hewn wood. A walk-in stone fireplace shelters a cast-iron stove and pillows, often occupied by the inn's cats. Oriental rugs on burnished wood floors along with comfortable sofas and chairs create a gracious aura. Here a breakfast is served of juice, cakes or muffins, quiche, fruit salad, granola and yogurt.

A climb up the spiral staircase brings you to two other bedrooms with arched windows and pitched ceilings, cozily furnished with quilted bedspreads and ruffled pillows. Balconies from one of these overlook both the deck and the living room. At the top of Blackthorne is the eagle's nest. Its eight sides are enclosed by multi paned floor-to-ceiling windows that look out to oak, redwood and bay trees. Its skylight offers a view of the stars, and a ladder leads up to the rooftop deck. This is not exactly your conventional inn.

BLACKTHORNE INN, 266 Vallejo Avenue (P.O. Box 712), Inverness, California 94937. Telephone: (415) 663-8621. Accommodations: five rooms with double or queen-size beds; two shared baths within the inn, one in outside bath house, all with showers; no telephones; no television. Rates: moderate, breakfast included. Children permitted on occasion. No pets. No smoking in guest rooms. Cards: MC, VISA. Open all year.

Getting There: From Highway 101 take Sir Francis Drake Boulevard through Olema towards Inverness. Turn left on Vallejo Avenue at the Inverness Park Grocery, two miles south of Inverness.

TLC in Turn-of-the-Century Style
GRAMMA'S BED AND BREAKFAST INN
Berkeley

There is no real Gramma here, but a large portrait of the owner's grandmother, Elizabeth Taber, hangs in the stairwell. She was an Irish immigrant who ran a boardinghouse in Boston. Kathy Kuhner has dedicated this inn to her and instigated some grandmotherly practices, such as keeping a cookie jar freshly stocked at all times.

Gramma's is located in a complex of turn-of-the-century buildings, a five-minute walk away from Berkeley's UC campus. The main house is a Tudor-style mansion. Most of the original beautiful detailing of the lower floor remains intact, such as the intricately inlaid hardwood floors and foliated plaster friezes. In the living room a graceful bay of leaded clear glass windows looks out to the big trees that screen the inn from busy Telegraph Avenue. In the rear are a second sitting room and a large breakfast area with enormous windows opening to a broad deck and bountiful gardens where a fountain bubbles away.

Rooms in the main house range from small to quite large, with sitting areas and window seats; one room has a private deck. In the rear of the garden, the former servants' quarters have been reconstructed into elegant accommodations with tiled fireplaces and windows on two sides. Recently Kathy acquired a Queen Anne Victorian next door with a carriage house in the rear, adding another ten guest rooms to the inn. The Queen Anne is a showplace with inlaid floors, hand-painted ceilings, marble fireplaces and stained-glass windows.

For breakfast Gramma's serves some of the best granola in town, along with fresh fruits, croissants, cereal and French roast coffee. On

Sundays the public is invited in for an elaborate champagne brunch that includes buffets of cold dishes, hot dishes and desserts, all prepared with great care. For inn guests, complimentary coffee and tea are available all day; wine and cheese are served in the evening Monday through Friday. And if you want to entertain at Gramma's, a greenhouse room will seat up to twenty-five for dinner.

GRAMMA'S BED AND BREAKFAST INN, 2740 Telegraph Avenue, Berkeley, California 94705. Telephone: (415) 549-2145. Accommodations: twenty-nine rooms with twin, double, queen- or king-size beds; all but two rooms have private baths with tub and/or shower; some rooms fully equipped for the handicapped; telephones; television on request. Rates: moderate to expensive, breakfast included. Open to the public for Sunday brunch. Children by special arrangement. No pets. Cards: MC, VISA. Facilities for weddings. Open all year.

Getting There: From San Francisco cross Bay Bridge and follow signs to Berkeley via Highway 80. Take Ashby Avenue exit east to Telegraph Avenue and turn left.

Rebirth of a Former State Capital
BENICIA

Benicia was founded in 1846 on the Carquinez Straits, where the Sacramento and San Joaquin rivers flow into San Francisco Bay. During the gold rush the city's strategic location brought such prosperity that the town rivaled San Francisco as a commercial center, and for a year in the 1850s Benicia was the capital of California. It was also the site of a major United States Army arsenal and so noted for its educational institutions that it was dubbed the Athens of California. Then history and commerce bypassed Benicia, resulting in a rare phenomenon—an entire nineteenth-century town largely intact, possessing some of the most significant buildings of California's early history.

Today Benicia is enjoying a renaissance, as both a growing suburban community and a mecca for antique hunters and lovers of history. Along First Street, the center of Benicia's Old Town, you'll find numerous antique shops, crafts studios and art galleries. And almost every weekend features some sort of celebration—parades, handicraft fairs and a peddlers' fair in August that brings some three hundred antique dealers to the town. Year-round attractions include fishing, cycling, bird watching and strolling around the historic buildings of this nineteenth-century town.

Getting There: From San Francisco, take Highway 80 northeast to Vallejo and Highway 780 southeast to the downtown Benicia exit. Turn left on Second Street, turn right on Military and then turn left on First Street, which leads to Old Town.

CAPTAIN DILLINGHAM'S INN
Benicia

Shipping and ship building were major industries in Benicia's heyday, and many sea captains made the town their home. One of these was William W. Dillingham, who booked lodgings with the widow Jane Paladini. He eventually married his landlady and enlarged her home, which was originally built in the 1850s. The Dillingham residence became a center for the town's social life and was owned by their heirs until 1981.

Benicia booster Roger Steck and some partners bought the house, built a two-story addition in the rear and opened Captain Dillingham's Inn in 1985. Steck had owned an antiques business and bought many pieces from Brian O'Neil, an American dealer living in Austria who came to Benicia to manage the inn. Lo and behold, O'Neil found many of the antiques he had exported among the furnishings—authentic and unusual pieces from ports of call around the world. In fact, each bedroom is decorated in a different theme—Arabic, French, Spanish, Chinese and such—as if a roving sea captain had collected these treasures during his journeys.

In one room you will find a gaudy wall hanging that was once the interior of a Bedouin tent. A rare collection of framed navigational charts from the 1800s distinguishes another room. And in another there's a headboard from Brittany with a curtained opening; originally this was the entrance to an enclosed bed. One of the nicest bedrooms is the former parlor of the old house, which boasts a beautiful onyx fireplace and a large Jacuzzi tub. In the new wing, french doors open from the rooms to a deck or a brick patio, which face a large garden abloom with marigolds and zinnias in summertime, mums in the fall. The upstairs rooms have cathedral ceilings, one with a skylight, and all are equipped with standard-size Jacuzzi tubs.

Hand-pegged plank floors of cherry wood gleam in the handsome breakfast room, which is graced by a twelve-foot-long refectory table from France. In the morning a buffet (once the end piece of an English hunt table) holds a selection of fresh fruit, breads, pastries, cereals, granola and marinated veggies, such as artichokes and cauliflower and pickled beets. Guests may eat here or outside at umbrella-topped tables on the multitiered decks, brick patio and adjacent gazebo. This area, which will comfortably accommodate over a hundred people, is very popular for weddings.

Behind the house is a small grove of gnarled eucalyptus trees that recalls another little-known chapter from Benicia's seafaring days. No trees grew in the town until a local priest organized the sea captains to bring back saplings from their travels. Thus the exotic greening of Benicia.

CAPTAIN DILLINGHAM'S INN, 145 East D Street, Benicia, California 94510. Telephone: (707) 746-7164. Accommodations: ten rooms with twin, double, queen- and king-size beds; private baths, most with Jacuzzi tub; wheelchair access; telephones; television. Rates: moderate to expensive, breakfast included. Children over 14 welcome. No pets. Cards: AE, CB, DC, MC, VISA. Facilities for weddings and small conferences. Open all year.

Getting There: Proceed down First Street and turn left on East D.

Modern Amenities in an Historic Site
THE UNION HOTEL
Benicia

One of Benicia's restored buildings is the Union Hotel, built in 1882 not far from the water's edge. The interior of the three-story structure was rebuilt to provide comforts like modern tiled bathrooms, all with Jacuzzi tubs. Each of the twelve guest rooms is decorated around a different theme. There's Louis le Mad with tufted, gilted pseudo-French furnishings, Four Poster with a high Queen Anne canopy bed, Mei Ling with Chinese Chippendale, 1932 with metallic art deco pieces, Summer Skies with lilac walls and white wicker ware, and so forth. Many of the rooms have lovely views of Carquinez Bay and the bridge that arches over the straits. All are scented with potpourri.

A bar and a restaurant, Prevot's, occupy the first floor, separated from the street by floor-to-ceiling windows of stained and leaded glass. A handcarved 1886 bar lines one wall of the saloon, which is furnished with armchairs and love seats around low marble-topped tables. The hotel has no common room, so this saloon also serves as a salon for a complimentary Continental breakfast of orange juice, cream biscuits and coffee. Those wanting a heartier meal may order from an extensive à la carte selection at the restaurant.

THE UNION HOTEL, 401 First Street, Benicia, California 94510. Telephone: (707) 746-0100. Accommodations: twelve rooms with queen- or king-size beds; private baths with Jacuzzi tub/showers; telephones; color television. Rates: moderate to expensive, Continental breakfast included; lower rates on weeknights. Children welcome. No pets. Cards: AE, DC, MC, VISA. Open all year.

GOLD COUNTRY

Sacramento
The Mother Lode and Lake Tahoe

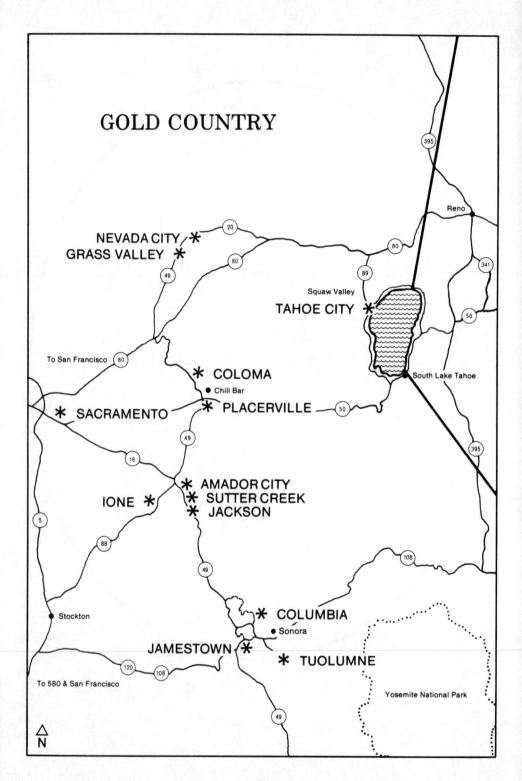

GOLD COUNTRY

NEVADA CITY
GRASS VALLEY
TAHOE CITY
Squaw Valley
Reno
To San Francisco
COLOMA
Chili Bar
SACRAMENTO
PLACERVILLE
South Lake Tahoe
AMADOR CITY
SUTTER CREEK
JACKSON
IONE
Stockton
COLUMBIA
Sonora
JAMESTOWN
TUOLUMNE
To 580 & San Francisco
Yosemite National Park
N

The Gateway to the Gold Country
SACRAMENTO

In 1839, when California was still part of Mexico, a Swiss adventurer named John Sutter obtained a Mexican land grant to establish the colony of Nuevo Helvetia at the spot where the American River flows from the Sierras into the Sacramento River. Here, the present site of Sacramento, he built Sutter's Fort with timber extracted from the nearby mountains. Then on January 24, 1848 at one of Sutter's sawmills in Coloma, James W. Marshall found some glittering specks in the mill tailrace. These turned out to be gold and the destiny of California was forever changed. Marshall rushed back to Sacramento to share his discovery with Sutter who agreed to keep the strike a secret. But the news leaked out and within the next decade some hundred thousand prospectors came to the Mother Lode, taking $550 million in ore from her rich veins.

Neither Sutter, who lost his holdings and was bankrupt by 1852, nor Marshall, who died a pauper, ever prospered from the Sierra mines. Among those who really struck it rich from the gold rush were the merchants of Sacramento, where the miners came to spend their diggings. Four of the wealthiest shopkeepers—Charles Crocker, C. P. Huntington, Mark Hopkins and Leland Stanford—later turned their profits into gigantic fortunes by starting the Central Pacific and Southern Pacific railroads. In 1854 Sacramento became the capital of California and later the western terminus for the Pony Express.

Today the colorful early history of this city has been recaptured in Old Sacramento, a restoration and reconstruction of the old town along the river front. Here wooden sidewalks pass by the Huntington Hopkins Hardware Store, Pony Express terminus and the old Wells Fargo office, plus a bevy of restaurants and shops. Other tourist attractions in Sacramento include the Crocker Art Gallery, the Railroad Museum, the reconstruction of Sutter's Fort, riverboat cruises and, of course, the capitol itself and the many Victorian mansions that were built nearby. In a quiet area just east of the capitol several of these older homes have been turned into inns.

Getting There: From San Francisco Highway 80 leads to Sacramento; from Los Angeles, take Highway 5. Sacramento is served by Amtrak and a number of airlines, including AirCal, PSA, United and Western.

A Very Professional Inn for Particular People

THE BRIGGS HOUSE
Sacramento

Four dedicated women brought the bed and breakfast concept to Sacramento in 1981 when they bought a lovely 1901 Colonial Revival home near the capitol and within weeks transformed it into an inn. Their aim was to provide an old-fashioned homelike ambience for two types of clientele: the increasing number of tourists attracted by Old Sacramento, and business or professional travelers. The owners furnished the place with family antiques: Oriental rugs on the hardwood floors, lace curtains, crocheted, patchwork or quilted bedspreads and pretty printed sheets. A downstairs bedroom has a wood-burning fireplace, one of the upstairs units has a private sundeck and out back there's a rustic garden cottage with a fully equipped kitchen. The rooms are filled with fresh flowers and touches that make this a very special place: engraved stationery, bathrobes for the guests' use and hardbound diaries in each room where tenants record their impressions of the inn or their adventures in Sacramento.

The day begins with a full breakfast served on antique china either in your room, in the parlor or in the pretty rear garden, which is planted with camelias, firs and orange trees. In season, oranges from these trees provide the freshly squeezed juice for the morning meal. Croissants and homemade breads and jams are also served, along with the cook's daily creations—things like frittatas and baked apples with cinnamon sauce. At night there's no lack of things to do at Briggs House. Beverages, fruit and nuts are served before the fire in the early evening. A hot tub, an unusual sauna set in a wine cask, and a big hammock offer relaxation in the garden. And if you want to take a spin on a bicycle, the inn will provide that too.

Briggs House also presents occasional special events and theme weekends: musical entertainment, Sunday tea and crumpets, and a teddy bear sale, to name a few. There's a nominal charge for some of the sessions, but they are staged by professionals as is everything else at this superb inn.

BRIGGS HOUSE, 2209 Capitol Avenue, Sacramento, California 95816. Telephone: (916) 441-3214. Accommodations: five rooms with twin, double or queen-size beds; three rooms have private baths, two share baths, tub/showers and stall showers; cottage with two suites, one with full kitchen and private bath, one with fireplace, each sleeps four; telephones in some rooms; no television; air conditioned. Rates: moderate, breakfast included; government rates on week nights. Younger children welcome in garden cottage. No pets. No smoking in guest rooms. Cards: AE, MC, VISA. Open all year. Advance schedule of special events available upon request. Parlor available to guests for meetings or social events by special arrangement.

Getting There: Take 15th Street exit from Highway 80, turn right to 16th Street, turn left and stay on 16th until you reach Capitol Avenue. Turn right on Capitol.

Where the Gold Rush Began
EL DORADO COUNTY
Coloma and Placerville

Within months of James Marshall's discovery of gold at Coloma in January, 1848, thousands of fortune hunters were roaming the nearby mountains and rivers seeking *el dorado* (the gilt). One of the most popular camps, about seven miles south of Coloma, was named Dry Diggings because the miners had to tote the gravel that contained the ore to water for washing. But many of the rough and tough adventurers who inhabited the camp found an easier way to get their gold: murder and robbery became so rampant that a vigilante committee was formed to hang the culprits. And as the hangings increased the camp became known as Hangtown until a more respectable group of citizens changed it to Placerville.

In the early years of the gold rush both Coloma and Placerville thrived, and they became engaged in a heated rivalry for the county seat. Coloma, which had grown to a city of over ten thousand inhabitants within a few years of the gold strike, won out at first, but in 1857, after several heated elections, the county government was moved to Placerville, which was then the third largest city in California. Meanwhile, the gold in El Dorado County was being depleted and the fickle prospectors had moved on to the vast mines to the south and north. Placerville managed to prosper as a government and commercial center, but by 1868 Coloma had dwindled to a population of two hundred, among them a bitter and impoverished James Marshall, who survived by occasionally working as a gardener.

Coloma today, barely a speck on the map, is best known for its historic park that contains the reconstruction of Sutter's Mill where the gold was first discovered. Placerville, still a thriving town, contains a number of historic buildings and the old Gold Bug mine which is open to the public. Nearby attractions include white-water river rafting, a number of prize-winning wineries and Apple Hill® Farms, an association of forty-four independent apple growers whose farms on a mountain ridge east of Placerville are open to the public. In addition to selling apples, other fruits, vegetables and preserves, many of the farms have arts and crafts stores, bake shops and sandwich bars. Higher in the mountains a number of ski areas are located.

A Fishin' Hole and Balloon Rides, Too

COLOMA COUNTRY INN

Coloma

Few of Coloma's gold rush buildings are still standing, and these are secluded in a countryish area off Highway 49. One is a fine old 1856 farmhouse built by Hugh Miller, one of the town's early saloon keepers, just down the road from two 1850s churches that have also survived history. The old Miller house is now the Coloma Country Inn, owned and operated by Cindi and Alan Ehrgott, nostalgia buffs who came here from Pasadena for a holiday—and stayed.

The house is furnished with Early Americana, which Cindi has been collecting since she was fifteen (and she doesn't look a whole lot older today). "When I was in high school," she confesses, "I worked and saved all my money to buy antiques, while all of my girl friends were buying clothes." She is particularly proud of her collection of patchwork quilts, some over one hundred years old. One of these is hung on the wall of the library-living room, originally the summer kitchen, where a stunning assortment of old crocks, sugar buckets and other Early American crafts are also displayed. But the room is by no means cluttered; in fact, its pitched roof and the long raised hearth under the fireplace impart a feeling that is more contemporary than quaint.

The four bedrooms are done up in the same tasteful style. Most popular is the Lavender Room, splashed by sun from windows on three

sides, and containing a rare eight-piece set of hand-painted cottage furniture from the East Coast. "It's poor-man's Victoriana," Cindi explains. "People who couldn't afford walnut or oak just painted the pine."

The Ehrgotts serve late-afternoon refreshments by the fire or, on warm days, out in the gazebo, surrounded by pretty gardens. Breakfast (perhaps quiche, fruit and coffee) is brought to your room, if you like, or served in the formal dining room, where over the lace café curtains you can glimpse apple and persimmon trees and a small pond, where a canoe might lure you for a little morning fishing. But if you're truly adventurous, you will have already had your morning recreation: Alan Ehrgott is a licensed hot-air balloon pilot, and the inn offers special packages that feature a prebreakfast flight. If that's too daring for you and the pond is too tame, packages are also offered that include white-water rafting down the American River.

COLOMA COUNTRY INN, High Street (P.O. Box 502) Coloma, California 95613. Telephone: (916) 622-6919. Accommodations: four rooms with double beds and two shared baths; no telephones; no television. Rates: moderate, breakfast included. No children. No pets. No smoking. No credit cards. Open all year.

Getting There: From Placerville, take Highway 49 north. On the south edge of Coloma the highway makes a sharp turn to the right. Continue straight ahead on Church Street and turn right on High Street.

Watch the White Water Rush Past

RIVER ROCK INN
Chili Bar

During the 1850s the South Fork of the American River between Coloma and Placerville was heavily populated with miners. Today, it swarms with the rafts and kayaks of white-water aficionados who come from all over to enjoy the thrills of this very fast river and to see the relics of old mining camps en route. Chili Bar (a gold rush camp founded by Chilean miners) is headquarters for the river raft expeditions, and just a little downstream is River Rock Inn. This contemporary stone and brick house furnished with antiques was the country home of Dorothy Irvin, who has turned it into an inn.

All the rooms front on a wide deck with spectacular views of the river, which is illuminated by floodlight at night. (The bed heights were designed to be eye level with the river.) Chaises, tables, a hot tub and potted flowers grace the deck, where breakfast is served on sunny mornings. On chilly days the morning repast is taken before a fire in the stone-walled dining room—and a bounteous meal it is. Dorothy on a typical day might serve orange juice mixed with bananas, eggs Benedict, apple crêpes, freshly baked rolls and baking powder biscuits, homemade jams and fresh fruit. In fact, one might say she is a compulsive cook. The big country kitchen is the hub of this house and there usually are cookies, pies or cakes baking in the oven—for the guests' enjoyment—while bread rises on an ancient wood-burning cookstove. By special arrangement she will prepare dinners or picnic lunches for her guests.

Dorothy will also arrange for one- or two-day raft trips down the river, conducted by qualified guides. For the less adventurous, there's excellent trout and white salmon fishing on the banks near the inn. And if you're truly lazy, you can just lie on the deck and watch the white water rush by.

RIVER ROCK INN, 1756 Georgetown Drive, Placerville, California 95667. Telephone: (916) 622-7640. Accommodations: one two-room suite with private bath and queen-size bed; three rooms with double beds; one with private bath; others with half baths and shared shower; no telephones; color television; air conditioned. Rates: moderate, breakfast included. Children welcome. Pets discouraged. No credit cards. Open all year.

Getting There: From Placerville take Highway 49 (Coloma Road) north to the intersection of Highway 193 (Georgetown Road), which leads to Chili Bar. After crossing the American River turn left immediately on the first road, which leads to the inn.

Old Farmhouse Complete with Pastoral Setting

THE FLEMING JONES HOMESTEAD
Placerville

Among the hordes who rushed to the gold country in 1851 were Fleming Jones' parents, dairy farmers from Wisconsin. But instead of gold, they staked their claim on a homestead of ninety-seven wooded acres just east of Placerville. Fleming liked to gamble and also acquired an interest in a saloon. After one particularly good night at the tables, he arrived home with twelve hundred dollars and told his wife, Florence, to go build herself a house. She did. Descendants of the Jones family lived there until the late 1970s, and in 1980 the old farmhouse and eleven acres of the land were acquired by Janice Condit, who ever since has devoted her considerable energies to recreating an old-fashioned farm—the kind of place most of us dreamed of visiting when we were kids.

You enter through the farmhouse kitchen, rife with the aroma of freshly baked bread or simmering preserves of fruit from the pear, apple and fig trees in the surrounding orchards. A homey parlor is furnished with a well-used Steinway grand and an old church pump organ. In the adjoining dining room, a massive oak table with carved griffin feet is set for breakfast with gold-rimmed Haviland and Limoges china. And a hearty farm breakfast it is: homemade hot muffins, baked apples, Janice's preserves and breads (frequent blue-ribbon winners at the county fair) and eggs minutes-fresh from the chicken roost.

Four of the guest rooms are located in the 1883 farmhouse and two in the recently restored bunkhouse. Furnishings include cast-iron or carved-oak bedsteads (equipped with *new* matresses, flowered quilts and matching sheets). Children's school desks, topped with vases of fresh flowers, serve as nightstands.

A favorite pastime of Homestead guests is helping with the farm chores: feeding the chickens and ducks, collecting eggs, helping to tend the vegetable gardens or harvest the fruit from the trees, or petting Janice's Welsh pony and miniature Shetland. Other guests prefer just to loaf on the porch swing, throw the ball for Rocky (the tireless fetching dog) and admire the view of the rolling, wooded countryside.

FLEMING JONES HOMESTEAD, 3170 Newtown Road, Placerville, California 95667. Telephone: (916) 626-5840. Accommodations: six rooms with double beds (two of these also have singles at an extra charge; some private baths, some shared, tub/shower, shower and big

The Fleming Jones Homestead

old tubs; some rooms wheelchair accessible; no telephones; no television. Rates: moderate, breakfast included. Children 12 and over welcome; younger please inquire. No pets. No credit cards. Open all year.

Getting There: From Placerville, take Highway 50 east to the Newtown Road/Point View Drive exit. At the base of the off ramp, jog to the right to another stop sign and turn left onto Broadway, which runs parallel to the freeway and becomes Newtown Road. The Homestead is on the right just past a pond.

Where the Vines Have Replaced the Mines
AMADOR COUNTY
Amador City, Sutter Creek and Jackson

Located in the heart of the Mother Lode, this is one of California's smallest counties in both size and population, yet its mines yielded more than half the gold that came out of the entire Sierra foothills. Gold may still be panned in the streams, and many of the old mines are open to the public. But today the commercial interests of the Amadoreans have turned from the mines to the vines. Amador County's Shenandoah Valley produces some of the state's most distinctive Zinfandel. And many of the wineries are open for touring and winetasting.

In Amador County, Highway 49 winds through oak-studded hillsides and the old mining towns of Amador City, Sutter Creek and Jackson. The brick or clapboard buildings, with their second-story balconies covering raised sidewalks, now house antique shops, art and craft galleries, and saloons. A worthwhile side trip from Sutter Creek or Jackson is a visit to the picturesque mining town of Volcano, situated in a valley surrounded by pine-forested mountains above Highway 49.

It would be difficult to become bored in Amador County. Besides shopping, sightseeing, mine and wine touring, and visiting historic museums, you may participate in a host of recreational activities. There are fishing and boating at nearby Amador, Pardee and Camanche lakes, and rafting on the Mokelumne River. There are hunting, tennis, a nine-hole golf course, and even skiing in nearby Kirkwood Meadows. And on summer evenings the Claypipers Theater presents old-time melodrama. You can also eat well in Amador County. Jackson offers a number of family-style Italian restaurants, such as Buscaglia's, where the food is both hearty and above average.

Getting There: From San Francisco take Highway 580 east through Tracy to Manteca, Highway 99 north to Stockton and Highway 88 northeast to Jackson. Sutter Creek is four miles north of Jackson on Highway 49; Amador City is two miles north of Sutter Creek. This part of the Mother Lode may also be reached by taking Highway 50 to Placerville and proceeding south on Highway 49.

Now a Treasure Trove of Antiques

THE MINE HOUSE
Amador City

Over $23 million in gold bullion was removed from the Keystone Consolidated Mines in Amador City before they were finally closed in 1942. The mining company's offices, grinding and assay rooms were located in a two-story brick building on a hillside across the highway from the mines. In 1954 the building, then abandoned and run down, was purchased by Marguerite and Peter Daubenspeck, who came to California on a vacation, were charmed by Amador City and decided to stay. They restored the old mine as an inn, now run by their son Peter Daubenspeck III and his wife, Ann Marie.

The Daubenspecks furnished the entire building with authentic period furniture, found within one hundred miles of Amador City. And the rooms are handsome, indeed. There are burled walnut pieces, Empire dressers, commodes topped with Italian marble, rockers, platform rockers, armoires, carved bedsteads, and under each bed an old-fashioned bed warmer. Many of the rooms contain old pitchers and wash basins set on a commode. But these are for show only. You will find modern wood-paneled bathrooms throughout.

The rooms of the Mine House are named after their original usage. Downstairs is the Mill Grinding Room, where the ore was brought to be ground; the supports that held the shafts for the grinding machinery are still on the ceiling. Next door is the Assay Room, where the ore was evaluated for its gold content. There is also a Stores Room that once contained the mining supplies. All the interiors are of painted brick.

The upstairs rooms, however, are the most attractive, with thirteen-foot-high ceilings paneled in redwood. On one side, rooms open to a wide balcony overlooking the highway. On the other side they open to a covered patio dug out of the grassy hillside. These rooms

141

originally housed the Keystone Consolidated Mining Company's offices and are appropriately named: Directors' Room, Bookkeeping Room, Keystone Room and Vault Room, which contains the safe in which the bullion was stored until the stagecoach transported it to San Francisco.

Back on the first floor, the former retort room, where the gold was smelted into bullion, now serves as a parlor for guests and also as an art gallery for the paintings of Ann Marie and other local artists. In warm weather you can also relax by the swimming pool behind the inn. And in the morning, you'll find a tray of orange juice, sweet rolls and hot beverages by your door.

THE MINE HOUSE, P.O. Box 245, Amador City, California 95601. Telephone: (209) 267-5900. Accommodations: seven rooms with one or two double beds; private baths with showers; no telephones; no television. Rates: inexpensive, breakfast tray included. Children welcome. No pets. No credit cards. Open all year.

Getting There: The Mine House is on Highway 49 in Amador City.

Mother Inn of the Mother Lode
SUTTER CREEK INN
Sutter Creek

Here, in a century-old, two-story house in the heart of Sutter Creek, California's first bed and breakfast inn was opened nearly two decades ago. Jane Way fell in love with the house, once the biggest in town, on a visit to the Mother Lode in 1966. The house was not for sale, but after months of perseverance she convinced the owners to allow her to buy it, and soon her bed and breakfast shingle was inviting travelers to spend the night. Word spread and later many of the visitors included would-be innkeepers who borrowed her ideas and incorporated them into their own places. Sutter Creek is truly the prototype of a California country inn.

Jane, a woman of enormous talent and energy, has dressed up every inch of the inn with a riot of color and charm. The gracious living room, painted a pale aqua, is comfortably furnished with large sofas upholstered in floral print, a hutch filled with antique china, a small piano and a grandfather clock. A chess set by the fireplace and a tray of homemade cookies and lemonade or coffee await your enjoyment.

142

Sutter Creek Inn

But the highlight of a stay at Sutter Creek Inn is breakfast in the country-kitchen/dining room. Walls, partially brick, partially paneled, are hung with copper colanders, an Oriental rug and a collection of guns. Two long, polished plank tables are gaily set with orange mats, gold-rimmed china and a pewter pitcher filled with dried flora. Shuttered windows look out to the lawn and gardens. Jane's menu is ambitious: fresh fruit, berries or perhaps peaches, just picked from the inn's own trees, along with pancakes full of chopped nuts and apples, corn bread or a soufflé.

Several upstairs bedrooms in the main house have recently been enlarged. But the most desirable rooms are the outbuildings in the rear of the house—the woodshed, carriage house, storage shed and old laundry house, which Jane has extensively remodeled and furnished with flair. Eight of these have fireplaces and four have "swinging beds," actually suspended by cables from the ceiling. This was an idea she picked up in the tropics of Mexico where people often hang their beds to avoid crawling insects and lizards. But if you suffer from motion sickness, you won't need Dramamine; the beds may be stabilized easily.

No two of the rooms are alike, except that they are perfectly appointed down to the tiniest details: books, magazines, a deck of cards, whatever. In one you might find a fireplace, in another a Franklin stove, in yet another a sunken bathtub. Some open out to private patios or porches, others into the lovely back garden. Some are furnished in solid Early American maple, others have canopied four-poster beds, still others contain brightly painted wicker ware. Jane transforms whatever she finds around the countryside: an old drum topped with a wicker tray for a table, a miner's scale for a planter, a milk can for a lamp base, two water barrels for the base of a bathroom sink. All is visual joy.

Though there is much to see and do in the Sutter Creek area, Jane admits that most of her guests come primarily to relax, to get away from it all. But one diversion unique to this inn is a session of Jane's handwriting analysis, made with the warning: "This might change your life completely." So might a visit to Sutter Creek Inn.

SUTTER CREEK INN, 75 Main Street (P.O. Box 385), Sutter Creek, California 95685. Telephone: (209) 267-5606. Accommodations: seventeen bedrooms with twin, double and queen-size beds; all private baths; no telephones; no television. Rates: moderate, breakfast included; lower rates on weeknights. Children discouraged; children under 15 not allowed. No pets. No credit cards. Open all year except Thanksgiving, Christmas and Christmas Eve.

Where Modern Comforts Mingle with Antique Artifacts
THE HANFORD HOUSE
Sutter Creek

A two-story brick building on the northern edge of Sutter Creek looks like a restored relic from the gold rush days. Actually, it's only a few years old, but behind it is an old Spanish adobe that serves as nucleus of The Hanford House. The builder of the complex aspired to mix the old with the new, but there was an impersonal feeling about the inn when it first opened in 1983. A year later retired stockbroker Jim Jacobus and his wife Lucille acquired the inn and gave it a warm and homey ambience. "We feel as though we have been innkeepers forever," says Lucille.

The old adobe with its whitewashed walls and high beamed ceiling houses the comfortably furnished parlor, with books and magazines spread out on the coffee table. But creatures other than inngoers inhabit this room: a gigantic teddy bear sits in a chair by the door and all around are stuffed bears of various sizes and shapes. "We never really collected teddy bears," Jim recalls, "but our son's girl friend brought one to the inn as a gift. Then all our guests thought we collected bears and sent them to us." The menagerie of teddys now spreads throughout the premises.

In the rear another new brick wing houses the guest rooms. These contain new queen-size beds with, in most rooms, headboards fashioned from antique doors, luxurious modern baths and European or American furnishings that in some cases date back to the eighteenth century. All the rooms are air-conditioned or carpeted. And each contains those often-neglected touches that insure a relaxing stay: four pillows on the

bed, reading lamps on each side of the bed, a comfortable couch or two armchairs, plants and fresh flowers. On the top floor of the bedroom wing a large deck commands a panoramic view of the town of Sutter Creek and the surrounding hills. Upstairs there is also a deluxe—and more expensive—unit with a view and a fireplace with gas-burning logs.

Back in the old adobe, breakfast is served at small tables in the dining area; juice, fruit, cheese, and muffins or sweet rolls are usually offered. You might want to read the morning paper, but you will be distracted by the writing on the walls. From floor to ceiling are inscriptions to the Jacobuses from grateful guests. In fact, this three-dimensional guest book has overflowed onto the ceiling. You'll need a ladder at checkout time.

HANFORD HOUSE, 3 Hanford Street (P.O. Box 847), Sutter Creek, California 95685. Telephone: (209) 267-0747. Accommodations: nine rooms with queen-size beds; private baths with tub/shower; one room with facilities and tub for the handicapped in bathroom plus wheelchair access; no telephones; no television. Rates: moderate to expensive, breakfast included; discount on weeknights. No children. No pets. Some designated no-smoking rooms. Cards: MC, VISA. Facilities for small conferences. Open all year.

A Romantic Place for Romantic Occasions
FOXES IN SUTTER CREEK
Sutter Creek

Pete and Min Fox had absolutely no intention of becoming innkeepers when they bought this 130-year-old house on Sutter Creek's Main Street in 1979. Pete moved his real estate office there and Min operated her antique business downstairs. Then, one at a time, they started lavishly redecorating the rooms with Min's antiques and taking in guests. Finally, they built a carriage house in the back, with three more high-ceilinged rooms that, while new, recapture the aura of the nineteenth century. Lo and behold, the Foxes now have a full-fledged inn. "One advantage of turning an antique store into an inn," Min laughs, "is that you don't have to buy a lot of furniture." Only four pieces were purchased for the new annex.

The furnishings are exquisite and mostly authentic, such as an 1807 French armoire and a gilt Louis XV daybed in the Blue Room and a nineteenth-century carved Austrian bedroom set in the Anniversary

146

The Foxes

Suite. Some of the rooms have fireplaces, and even the bathrooms are romantic, many with claw-legged tubs and pedestal sinks, but with modern stall showers as well. Min has strewn the inn with dramatic bouquets of silk flowers and a collection of "foxy" artifacts. You might even find a pair of furry stuffed foxes cuddled up on your bed.

In each room, a table is set where breakfast is brought on silver trays. Or you can also be served in a little side patio that's especially pretty when the garden is ablaze with pink dogwood. There's a formal parlor in the front of the inn and a dining room, but most guests prefer to congregate in a homey seating area in the huge kitchen, while Min cooks up a storm. She gives her guests a number of choices among juices, hot beverages and four kinds of muffins; she often serves coddled eggs. "But we've done just about everything—sourdough french toast, eggs Benedict, even biscuits and pan gravy at a customer's request," Min recollects. She also likes to know when guests are celebrating a special occasion—honeymoon, anniversary or birthday—so she can plan a special surprise for them. Though nowadays she often knows without being told, as more and more of the honeymooners return for their anniversaries.

FOXES IN SUTTER CREEK, 77 Main Street, Sutter Creek, California 95685. Telephone: (209) 267-5882. Accommodations: six rooms with queen-size beds; private baths with stall showers or tub/shower; no telephones; color television available on request in carriage house. Rates: expensive, breakfast included; lower rates on week nights. No children. No pets. No smoking. Cards: AE, MC, VISA. Open all year.

The House of One Hundred Clocks
GATE HOUSE INN
Jackson

It wasn't just the miners who reaped the riches of the Mother Lode. Workers at the mines outside of Jackson used to tote their ore to the Chichizola General Store to exchange it for food, clothing and supplies. With this fortune gleaned from the gold rush, the Chichizola family at the turn of the century built a handsome two-story home next to the store, surrounded by a huge parcel of wooded, hilly acreage that is still owned by their descendants. Frank and Ursel Walker bought the house and opened the doors for bed and breakfast in 1981.

The original floral wallpaper still remains in mint condition in the

The Gate House Inn

master bedroom, which is cheered by a white tile fireplace. All the light fixtures are the original Italian imports, as is the marble fireplace in the living room. *Fin de siècle* antiques decorate all the rooms, along with fresh flowers and the Walkers' collection of over one hundred priceless old clocks. The choice quarters in the house, oddly enough, are the rooms, now a suite, formerly occupied by the Chichizolas' baby and cook. The cook's room, paneled in natural wood, has a bank of windows looking over the inn's pretty garden and orchards and a private staircase to the kitchen, which today provides a convenient exit to the inn's lovely swimming pool.

In the garden a grape arbor leads to the summerhouse, once the caretaker's cottage. There's a cast-iron wood-burning stove in the bedroom/sitting room and an immense cedar-paneled bathroom where the Walkers have installed stained-glass windows from the Comstock mansion in Virginia City. Across the lawn from this cottage, a screened-in barbecue area is provided for the guests' use should they tire of the hearty fare of Jackson's famous Italian family-style restaurants, which are within walking distance of the inn. You won't go hungry at breakfast either: the Walkers, who also own a restaurant in Sutter Creek, feed their guests well. The large table in the formal dining room is set with bone china, lace and linens and a rose on each napkin, and promptly at nine o'clock you are served a repast of juice, fresh fruits, pastries, muffins and coddled eggs.

GATE HOUSE INN, 1330 Jackson Gate Road, Jackson, California 95642. Telephone: (209) 223-3500. Accommodations: three bedrooms plus one suite and one cottage; queen-size beds; private baths with tub/shower or stall shower; no telephones; no television. Rates: moderate, breakfast included. No children. No pets. No smoking. No credit cards. Open all year.

Getting There: Turn off Highway 49 on Jackson Gate Road, just north of the intersection with Highway 88 from Stockton.

A Legacy of the Old South

THE HEIRLOOM

Ione

The Ione Valley, west of Highway 49 in the lower foothills, was the supply center for the boom towns of Amador County during the gold rush. This valley had been settled in the early 1800s by a number of Virginians, most of whom left during the Civil War. One family among these settlers, the Stephenses, left a legacy of the Old South: a brick antebellum mansion adorned with classical columned porticos. In 1980 Patricia Cross and Melisande Hubbs, two women whose children were grown, bought this architectural heirloom and turned it into an inn.

From a nondescript residential area you approach the Heirloom via a long driveway bordered by acacias, eucalyptuses and fruit trees— suddenly, a secret garden from another era. A giant gnarled wisteria, graceful magnolias, a brick terrace and a lush lawn nestle up to the gracious old house. A croquet course and hammocks are set up for guests. From the veranda you enter a spacious sitting room appointed with a square piano (once owned by Lola Montez), comfortable couches placed by the fireside, antiques, scattered Oriental rugs, and tables equipped with dominoes and jigsaw puzzles. A breakfast of fresh fruit, Louisiana dark-roast coffee and an entrée such as crêpes, quiche or soufflé is served here, in the garden, on a balcony or in one of the four upstairs bedrooms. These are decorated with irresistible charm, using family antiques from the innkeepers' former homes, brass bedsteads with flowered or patchwork quilts and fresh flowers. Two of these rooms open to a broad balcony. One has a fireplace, along with its own private entrance, bath and balcony. A recent addition is a two-room adobe cottage with wood-burning stoves and skylights.

THE HEIRLOOM, 214 Shakeley Lane (P.O. Box 322), Ione, California. Telephone: (209) 274-4468. Accommodations: six rooms with twin, double, queen- and king-size beds; three rooms share bath, three have private bath; no telephones; no television. Rates: moderate, breakfast included. No children under ten. No pets. No credit cards. Open all year.

Getting There: From Highway 49 take Highway 124 or Highway 88 west to Ione. Turn left on Main Street, turn right on Preston and left on Shakeley Lane.

CITY HOTEL
FALLON HOTEL
Columbia

Columbia was one of the most prosperous gold rush towns, with ore taken from its fabulously rich mines valued at over $80 million. Within three years after gold had been discovered in 1850 at Hildreth's Diggings, as it was then called, the town's population had grown to some twenty thousand and ranked as the second largest city in California. In its heyday Columbia boasted forty saloons, one hundred fifty gambling houses, eight hotels, four banks and two volunteer fire companies! Despite the latter's efforts, most of the original frame structures were destroyed in two early fires and the town was almost completely rebuilt in brick.

The Columbians' paranoia about fire has benefited posterity. The durability of these brick buildings prompted the state of California to purchase the town in 1945 and restore it as the Columbia Historic State Park. Today, except for an onslaught of tourists, the tree-shaded Main Street with its boardwalks and balconied buildings looks much the way it did in the 1860s. No automobiles are allowed in the town itself, but a stagecoach does lumber through, offering visitors a ride. The old blacksmith shop, harness and saddle shop, carpenter shop and a Chinese herb store are in working condition. And the state also restored two of Columbia's historic hostelries—the City and Fallon hotels. They are both operated by the Hospitality Management Program at Columbia Junior College as on-the-job training sites.

The first to be restored (for some $800,000) was the City Hotel, with its wrought-iron balconies overhanging the sidewalk of Main Street. Built in 1856, the hotel was ravaged by fire in 1867 and rebuilt four years later. The bedrooms have been impeccably furnished with massive burled-wood Victorian bedsteads framing comfortable brand-new mattresses, brass coatracks, and marble-topped bureaus. An upstairs parlor, reserved for guests' use, is stocked with books and games.

Downstairs are the What Cheer Saloon and a gracious high-ceilinged dining room, a serene setting for the magnificently appointed tables set with cut-glass goblets, graceful wineglasses of varying sizes, flowered service plates, small brass hurricane lamps and even silver napkin rings on the sparkling white napery. The food here is far removed from the mountain-country cooking you might expect to find in the Mother Lode. The City Hotel's kitchen is run by a professional chef and his

City Hotel

sophisticated, classical French menu would come as no surprise in New York or Paris. Now it's really no surprise in Columbia, either, because the restaurant has become well established as one of Northern California's finer dining places.

In 1986 a $3.5 million restoration of the Fallon Hotel was completed and the rooms were decorated in an ornate high-Victorian style that is more gay nineties than gold rush. The hotel is located next to the Fallon House Theatre, which is now the year-round home of the Columbia Actors Repertory.

At both hotels, the student staffers are attired in nineteenth-century dress. Both places also serve a light breakfast of orange juice and freshly baked breads, muffins and rolls. Rooms have only half baths, but the trip down the hall to the shower is made as pleasant as possible: the management thoughtfully provides each guest with a "bathroom caddy," a basket containing soap, washcloth, shower cap and even terrycloth shower shoes.

CITY HOTEL, P.O. Box 1870, Columbia, California 95310. Telephone: (209) 532-1479. Accommodations: nine rooms with twin, double and twin double beds; private half baths, community showers; no telephones; no television. Rates: moderate, Continental breakfast included. Open to the public for lunch, Sunday brunch and dinner. Children welcome. No pets. Cards: AE, MC, VISA. Conference facilities for 25 to 50 available. Open all year except Christmas and Christmas Eve.

FALLON HOTEL, P.O. Box 1870, Columbia, California 95310. Telephone: (209) 532-1470. Accommodations: thirteen rooms with twin, double and twin double beds; private half baths, community showers; one room wheelchair accessible; no telephones; no television. Rates: inexpensive to moderate, Continental breakfast included. Children welcome. No pets. No smoking in guest rooms. Cards: AE, MC, VISA. Facilities for conferences and weddings. Open all year.

Getting There: From San Francisco, 580 to Tracy, 205 to Manteca; Highway 120 east past Knights Ferry to intersection of Highway 108: Highway 108 east to Sonora; Highway 49 north to Columbia.

Hollywood's Favorite Old West Setting

JAMESTOWN

The gold rush came to Tuolumne County in 1848 when a seventy-five-pound nugget was discovered in Woods Creek, which once flowed down Jamestown's Main Street. Hordes of prospectors swarmed to the area, among them Colonel George James, a Philadelphia lawyer and veteran of the Mexican War, who founded and later skipped the town, deeply in debt to suppliers and employees. So embittered were the local folk that they renamed the town American Camp, but the original name of Jamestown was soon revived, and later it became a bustling railroad center. Today "Jimtown" is one of the most picturesque sights in the Mother Lode with the balconied facades of the old buildings overhanging raised wooden sidewalks. Movie fans will recognize the typical old west town as the site of *High Noon, Duel in the Sun* and *Butch Cassidy and the Sundance Kid.* Another hundred feature films were shot on the line of the Sierra Railway, whose steam-powered locomotives now pull trainloads of tourists through the oak-studded Sierra foothills. The railway depot is in Jamestown's Railtown 1897, now a State Historic Park with a twenty-six-acre roundhouse and shop complex where vintage rolling stock is exhibited. You can even pan for gold near Jamestown today; prospecting expeditions are conducted daily from the old livery stable on Main Street. And your nostalgic visit here is made complete by a stay in one of the town's restored hotels.

Getting There: From San Francisco, take 580 east to Tracy, then go east on 205 to Manteca; Highway 120 east to Highway 108 which leads east to Jamestown.

A Ten-Year Restoration Project

NATIONAL HOTEL

Jamestown

Built in 1859, the National has been continuously operated as a hotel except for a year in the mid-1920s when the old wooden structure was destroyed by fire and rebuilt in concrete. In 1974 the Willey brothers bought the place and, with Stephen Willey as resident manager, started a decade-long restoration. With a shoestring budget, Steve did most of the construction work himself. "When we ran out of money, we stopped.

When we got some more, we did more work." New plumbing, wiring and air conditioning were first priorities and the "cosmetics" came last.

One of these latter-day cosmetics was the reconstruction of the facade and the ornate redwood balcony, which overhangs the sidewalk, to match photos from the 1800s. The recently completed reception area adjoins the big downstairs saloon, resplendent with its massive original bar and an 1882 cash register. Upstairs the eleven bedrooms are decorated with antique lamps and nightstands, but the beds, with their brass steads, are blessedly new, as are the modern baths.

The two downstairs dining rooms have also been redecorated and are open to the public for lunch and dinner, serving everything from "gazpacho to escargots." In the morning, hotel guests are served a Continental breakfast of fruit, bread and coffee, along with that morning's *Chronicle*, either in the dining room or under the adjacent hundred-year-old grape arbor—the one thing that's not changed at the National.

NATIONAL HOTEL, Main Street (P.O. Box 502), Jamestown, California 95327. Telephone: (209) 984-3446. Accommodations: eleven rooms with twin and queen-size beds; some private and some shared baths with stall shower, wash basins in rooms without private baths; no telephones; television available on request. Rates: inexpensive, Continental breakfast included. Full bar service. Children over eight welcome. Some pets allowed. Cards: AE, MC, VISA. Open all year.

Younger Kid on the Block
JAMESTOWN HOTEL
Jamestown

Just down Main Street from the National Hotel is the Jamestown Hotel. They look as if they are the same age, but the Jamestown is the new kid on the block. It was actually built as a hospital in the 1920s, but in the late 1970s, the Sierra Railway started a restoration project to transform the place into a gold rush hotel.

A number of subsequent owners have added improvements. Now there are eight accommodations, mostly suites with a sitting room or two bedrooms with gaily papered walls and antique furnishings. Brass bedsteads, wicker settees and patchwork quilts abound. A bridge leads from a second-floor solarium to a spacious deck.

Jamestown Hotel

Downstairs a handsome saloon with swinging etched-glass doors is open to the public as is the attractive dining room for lunch and dinner. In the morning a Continental breakfast of fresh fruit and rolls is served here for guests only. But they will probably want to return for other meals as well. The menu is quite varied and the food is good.

JAMESTOWN HOTEL, Main Street (P.O. Box 539), Jamestown, California 95327. Telephone: (209) 984-3902. Accommodations: eight units including four suites with sitting rooms and three two-bedroom suites; twin, double and queen-size beds; private baths, tub/showers or stall showers; no telephones; no television. Rates: moderate, Continental breakfast included. Restaurant open for lunch and dinner. Full bar service. Children welcome. No pets. Cards: AE, MC, VISA. Open all year.

Victorian Replica on an Old Dairy Ranch
OAK HILL RANCH
Tuolumne

On an oak-studded knoll, surrounded by the pine forests of the lower Sierra, stands a Victorian replica that few could distinguish from the real thing. Sanford Grover, a retired college counselor, and his wife Jane, a former schoolteacher, built the four-bedroom house in 1979 as a family home and then decided to turn it into an inn. Although the structure is new, designed by their architect son, the details—a mahogany fireplace, redwood doors, an intricate staircase and many of the moldings—were collected by the Grovers for twenty-five years from old houses throughout California and as far away as Canada. They also did all the stripping and refinishing themselves.

The furnishings are period pieces and include a stunning burled walnut secretary and an old pump organ in the living room and a dining room table that seats twenty. Here the Grovers, dressed in turn-of-the-century attire, serve a hearty breakfast, cooked by themselves in the house's spacious country kitchen. A typical meal might be melon, an omelet with bacon, and biscuits with homemade jelly. "People who stay here are treated as our personal guests," Jane remarks.

Two of the upstairs rooms share an adjoining bath, complete with an old claw-legged tub and brass shower rail. A third room, furnished with a canopied bed, opens to a private balcony and shares the downstairs bath with the Rose Room, resplendent with Eastlake Victorian furnishings. Down the hill from the main house is a small

Oak Hill Ranch

cottage which was once a milking barn for this fifty-five-acre dairy ranch. The "cow palace," as it's known, has its own private living room with a large slate fireplace, a bedroom and complete kitchen. With a queen-size sofa bed in the living room and a roll-away bed, it will sleep five persons.

A Victorian gazebo and dance patio in the gardens have made Oak Hill a popular spot for weddings. The inn is often used as a site for small conferences. Although Oak Hill Ranch is but fifteen minutes away from Sonora, this is peaceful countryside with the quiet broken only by the sounds of cows, roosters, crickets and bullfrogs.

OAK HILL RANCH, 18550 Connally Lane (P.O. Box 307), Tuolumne, California 95379. Telephone: (209) 928-4717. Accommodations: four rooms with double or queen-size beds; two shared baths with tub/shower in main house; private bath and kitchen in cottage; no telephones; no television. Rates: inexpensive to moderate, full breakfast included. No children under 15. No pets. No smoking. No credit cards. Facilities for weddings and small conferences. Open all year.

Getting There: From Sonora take Highway 108 to Tuolumne Road. From there follow directions on map that will be sent to you when you make your reservations.

Queen Cities of the Northern Mines
NEVADA COUNTY
Nevada City and Grass Valley

At the peak of the gold rush Nevada City was the third largest town in California, with a population of twelve thousand. Today with only two thousand residents it's a much quieter place, except for a freeway that unfortunately cuts through its hilly streets. Despite a few misbegotten modern buildings, the town retains much of the character of an 1850s mining community, with picturesque gas lamps along the main street and many of the old buildings intact and restored. History buffs will find much of interest here. The American Victorian Museum, located in a former foundry, houses a collection of historical books, documents, photographs and old mining equipment. More history exhibits are mounted in the gingerbread-trimmed Firehouse No. 1 and at Ott's Assay Office, where the miners reportedly brought a booty of $27 million in ore over the years.

Five miles from Nevada City, in Grass Valley, California's richest mines once produced over $400 million in gold; a mining display with a thirty-one-foot waterwheel may still be viewed. Also open to the public are the homes of the infamous dancer Lola Montez and her young protégée, Lotta Crabtree, who later became nationally renowned as an actress. Four miles from Grass Valley is the semiabandoned town of Rough and Ready, which once tried to secede from the Union in protest of mining taxes.

This area is noted for a number of fine restaurants. Nearby lakes in the pine-forested mountains around the towns offer swimming and fishing. Good cross-country skiing is only twenty-five minutes away and the Sugar Bowl ski area is less than an hour's drive.

Getting There: From San Francisco take Highway 80 through Sacramento to Auburn. From here Highway 49 north leads to Grass Valley and Nevada City. From Reno take Highway 80 west to the intersection of Highway 20.

New Owners for a Gothic Beauty
RED CASTLE INN
Nevada City

This heavily ornamented, four-story brick structure has been cited as one of the best examples of gothic revival in the West. The imposing house was built between 1858 and 1860 as a two-family residence by Judge John Williams, who crossed the plains in 1849 and became a prominent businessman, mine owner and civic leader in Nevada City. The judge's son and his family also occupied the house and, according to local lore, young Williams, a lawyer, used to serenade the townsfolk every Sunday afternoon from the top veranda of the Red Castle with impromptu recitals on the trumpet or cornet.

The Red Castle has been operated as an inn since 1963 by several different owners. The latest are architect Conley Weaver and his wife Mary Louise, who took over in 1986. They have kept much of the former decor, but are slowly adding their own touches such as a pump organ in the living room, huge ficus trees here and there, and a croquet court in the woodsy garden. Mary Louise has also started serving afternoon tea with home-baked goodies like Scotch shortbread and has enlarged the breakfast to a generous spread including orange juice, muffins and breads, fruit compote and usually a hot casserole dish. This is set out

161

Red Castle Inn

buffet style in the hall, and guests may eat where they please—in their rooms, at a table set up in the garden, or on the wide veranda.

Guest rooms occupy all four floors of the building. The furnishings are old-fashioned eclectic: you'll find lace curtains, four-posters, wing chairs, love seats, Oriental rugs and the like. All but two of the rooms have private baths, in which old-fashioned washbasins remain, but new stall showers have been added. From the spacious, high-ceilinged rooms on the lower floor, french doors open out to the veranda. The middle floor contains "parlor suites," each composed of a tiny iron wood-burning stove, and a bedroom almost entirely filled by a double bed. Two garret rooms on the top floor have gothic windows and share a parlor, a bath and the balcony where Judge Williams' son conducted his concerts a century ago. From here and the lower verandas that surround the house, you look down on terraced, wooded gardens, and across to the picturesque town of Nevada City on the adjacent hillside.

RED CASTLE INN, 109 Prospect, Nevada City, California 95959. Telephone: (916) 265-5135. Accommodations: eight rooms with double beds; six rooms have private baths with shower, two rooms share a bath; no telephones; no television. Rates: inexpensive to moderate, breakfast included. Children discouraged. No pets. Smoking permitted in parlor only. No credit cards. Open all year.

Getting There: From Highway 49 take Broad Street exit in Nevada City; turn right to Sacramento Street, turn right again and proceed up hill to first road on the left; make a hard left turn onto Prospect Street.

Genial Hospitality in a Gold Baron's Home
MURPHY'S INN
Grass Valley

Innkeeping is no change of lifestyle for Marc Murphy. His family owned Murphy's Resort on the Russian River since 1902 and while in school he worked there every summer. After college he went into the real estate and construction business, but when the stately Edward Coleman house came on the market in 1982, he bought it to create an inn. Coleman's fortune was derived from the famous North Star and Idaho mines, as well as railroad and timber interests, and in 1866 he built his house to last forever. "It was in excellent shape," Marc recalls, with the original chandeliers, wainscoting and fireplaces in mint condition.

163

Murphy's Inn

There were only three owners before Murphy and they cared for the house with pride.

Nevertheless, with a nod to modern comforts, Marc added private baths for all but two of the eight bedrooms; some with copious double-spigoted showers for two. Several of the bedrooms have tile or marble fireplaces, as does the handsome parlor. After the inn had been open a year, Marc decided to serve a full breakfast, so he had an addition built to house a big cheerful kitchen with dining area. Now he can chat with his guests as he whips up a hearty breakfast that often changes. A typical feast would be fresh fruits and hand-squeezed juices, Belgian waffles, Polish sausage or coddled eggs, cottage fries and freshly ground coffee.

Marc has put together a wintertime ski package whereby his guests receive a $5 discount on lift tickets at Sugar Bowl, Monday through Friday, as well as $15 off their room rate at the inn. He also arranges golf specials in the summer and autumn.

MURPHY'S INN, 318 Neal Street, Grass Valley, California 95945. Telephone: (916) 273-6873. Accommodations: eight rooms with double, queen- or king-size beds, roll-away cots available; seven baths with stall shower or tub/shower; no telephones; no television; air conditioned; wheelchair access. Rates: moderate, breakfast included. Children over 10 welcome. No pets (will recommend local kennels). Smoking discouraged and not permitted in public areas. Cards: AE, MC, VISA. Open all year.

Getting There: From Highway 49 take Colfax exit. Turn left on South Auburn, then left on Neal.

Restrained Elegance Near a Mountain Lake
MAYFIELD HOUSE
Tahoe City

High above the Mother Lode, cradled among the peaks of the Sierra Nevada, lies Lake Tahoe: one of the most beautiful lakes in the world and one of California's most popular year-round playgrounds. This two-hundred-square-mile body of blue water is ringed by sandy beaches and forests of pine, cedar, dogwood and aspen. Swimming, boating and waterskiing lure the summer visitors, while excellent skiing—Squaw Valley and Heavenly Valley, for example—attract the winter tourist. The lake is bisected by the California-Nevada border, and all year hordes of gamblers flock to the Nevada casinos, which also offer big-name entertainment acts on a par with those of Las Vegas.

Far from the neon glitter of the casinos is the Mayfield House, on the edge of Tahoe City. This sturdy house was built of wood and stones among the pines in 1932 by Norman Mayfield, a contractor. A frequent guest was his good friend Julia Morgan, the architect responsible for the San Simeon castle of William Randolph Hearst. In 1980 the house was converted into an elegant little inn.

Signs of impeccable taste and an eye for detail pervade the inn, from the classical taped music in the living room to the restful rosy-beige and blue color scheme throughout, to thoughtful touches such as providing bathrobes for guests. The living room, with its dark-stained pine paneling, beamed ceiling and large stone fireplace, is furnished with Early American pine tables, chairs and love seats upholstered in blue, kerosene-fired hurricane lamps and an assortment of books and games. The adjoining breakfast room sports a corner hutch and some of the African violet specimens that abound throughout the house. Here a full breakfast is served on pretty blue and white flowered English china: homemade goodies such as Finnish pancakes or Portuguese toast with fruit sauce or cheese blintzes with berry sauce. Or, if you prefer, you may have your breakfast served your room.

All rooms are appointed with fresh flowers, a selection of books, down pillows and comforters, and original watercolors by Margaret Carpenter. Mullioned windows offer views of the mountains, woods or the golf course across the road. But each room has its distinctive decor.

From Mayfield House it's only a short walk to the beach for summer guests. In winter, skiing at Squaw Valley is about a fifteen-minute drive, but several smaller ski resorts are even closer. The casinos of Tahoe's North Shore can be reached in about fifteen minutes. And good restaurants are plentiful in the area.

MAYFIELD HOUSE, 236 Grove Street (P.O. Box 5999), Tahoe City, California 95730. Telephone: (916) 583-1001. Accommodations: six rooms with twin, queen- and king-size beds; three shared baths; no telephones; no television. Rates: moderate, breakfast included. No children under 10. No pets. Cards: MC, VISA. Open all year.

Getting There: From San Francisco or Reno take Highway 80 to Truckee, turn south on Highway 89 to Tahoe City, turn north on Highway 28 to Grove Street, turn left.

WINE COUNTRY

Sonoma, Napa and
The Russian River Valley

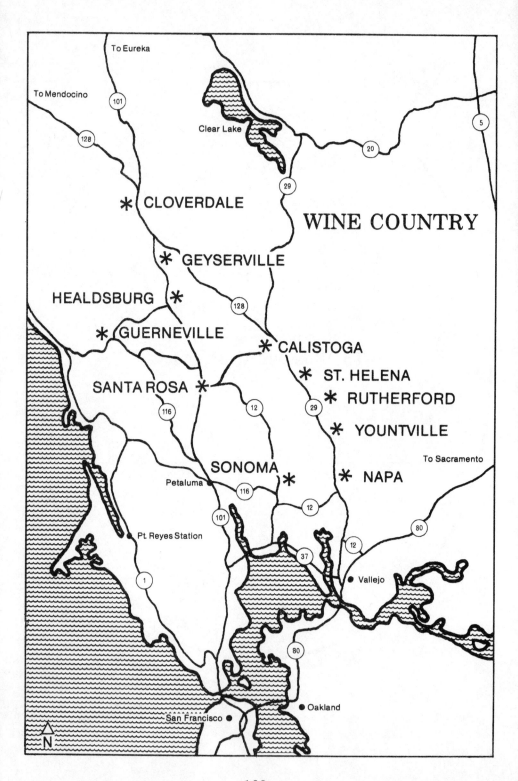

SONOMA

Sonoma's large tree-shaded plaza was laid out by General Mariano Guadalupe Vallejo in 1835 when he founded Pueblo de Sonoma as Mexico's most northerly outpost against hostile Indians. Twelve years earlier Mission San Francisco Solano de Sonoma had been built there as the northern tip of California's chain of missions. Vallejo built himself a two-story adobe *palacio* on the plaza where his regiment of Mexican soldiers marched daily. The peace was shattered on June 14, 1846, when a band of three dozen armed Americans, acting on their own authority, captured the town, imprisoned Vallejo, and proclaimed Sonoma capital of the Bear Flag Republic. The Bear Flag flew over the Sonoma plaza until the following month, when California became part of the United States.

Sonoma's second important settler after General Vallejo was Colonel Agoston Haraszthy, an Hungarian nobleman who planted his Buena Vista vineyards here in the 1850s and started northern California's winemaking industry. Sonoma has ever since been an important viticultural center. The Buena Vista's old stone cellars are open to the public. Tours are also conducted at the Sebastiani Winery, Hacienda Cellars, and twenty-nine other wineries in the area.

Sonoma is rich in Californiana. The Sonoma State Historic Park maintains the mission, General Vallejo's home and the Toscano Hotel, which are open to visitors. The old barracks, which has headquartered three armies—the Mexicans, the Bear Flag rebels and the Americans—has also been restored. Near Sonoma at Glen Ellen is the last home of Jack London, now also preserved as a state park.

Getting There: From San Francisco take Highway 101 north through San Rafael to Ignacio; there take Highway 37 east to Highway 21, which leads to Sonoma Plaza.

Overlooking the Historic Plaza
SONOMA HOTEL
Sonoma

At one corner of Sonoma's plaza is a three-story hotel. No one knows for certain when the hotel was built, but the lower two stories are probably a century-year-old adobe. The third floor with its high gables was added at a later date circa 1880, when the building housed a dry goods store on the first level and a two-story meeting hall above. About 1920 it was purchased by the winemaking Sebastiani family, who converted the cavernous hall into two floors, partitioned these into seventeen rooms and rechristened it the Plaza Hotel. In 1974 John and Dorene Musilli bought the hotel and redecorated it with antiques. "There's not one reproduction in the place," Dorene points out.

Sixteen of the rooms are furnished with French and English bedroom sets made at the turn of the century. In each room nearly all the pieces match—dresser, armoire, headboard, even chairs. Mattresses were custom-made to fit the odd-size beds, which were covered with quilted flowered spreads. Ruffled organdy curtains and a watering can full of dried flowers and grasses add a homey note to each room.

The seventeenth room has been named the Vallejo Room in honor of the Italianate hand-carved burled walnut furniture that belonged to General Vallejo's sister and is on loan to the hotel from the Sonoma League for Historic Preservation. The bed looks fit for the general himself, with an eleven-foot-high backboard and a bedspread of scarlet velvet.

The Musillis stripped eight coats of paint off the wainscoting in the hotel lobby to reveal the natural dark fir. Here, in front of a large stone fireplace, guests are served freshly squeezed orange juice, house-baked croissants and a choice of teas, coffee or hot chocolate. In 1982 the hotel's bar and restaurant was reopened and refurbished with antiques.

SONOMA HOTEL, 110 West Spain Street, Sonoma, California 95476. Telephone: (707) 996-2996. Accommodations: seventeen rooms with twin and double beds; some private baths with tub, community baths with showers; no telephones; no television. Rates: moderate, Continental breakfast included. Restaurant open to the public for lunch and dinner Friday through Tuesday; full bar. Children welcome. No pets. Cards: AE, MC, VISA. Open all year.

Sonoma Hotel

Romantic as a Bygone Era

VICTORIAN GARDEN INN

Sonoma

In the 1860s Sonoma was a tranquil town surrounded by prosperous farms and proud houses that relied on enclosed two-story towers topped by windmills for their water supply. In 1983 interior designer Donna Lewis transformed one of these farmhouses into a most romantic and sophisticated inn. The farmlands are long gone and subdivided, but nearly an acre of lush gardens and fruit trees remains, as does the old water tower (now *sans* windmill), which Donna has turned into three charming guest rooms. The top room has ten-foot ceilings and is decorated with a riot of blue and white Marimekko patterns: wallpaper, quilted spread, sheets, shower curtain and even the fabric gathered into shutter frames at the windows all match. For one of the downstairs rooms, Donna has chosen a pink and peach Laura Ashley print for the papers and fabric. In the other lower room a salmon and forest green floral pattern prevails. This room, the biggest and the best, boasts a brick wood-burning fireplace, high knotty-pine ceilings and redwood wainscoting. A forest green sofa assures comfortable seating here, as do wicker chairs in the other rooms.

Just a few steps away from the water tower, separated by a deck and grape arbor, is the old farmhouse with one guest room upstairs. Downstairs are the large living room, decorated in restful tones of beige, and the sunny, plant-filled dining area. Here Donna serves a "California breakfast," resplendent with fruits and unusual breads, or if you wish, wicker trays are available to carry your repast to one of the many tables out on the deck and gardens.

The Victorian Garden Inn offers nineteenth-century pastimes such as strolling in the gardens and playing lawn croquet. But it also offers a twentieth-century treat: a dip in the lovely swimming pool behind the house.

VICTORIAN GARDEN INN, 316 East Napa Street, Sonoma, California 95476. Telephone: (707) 996-5339. Accommodations: four rooms with double or queen-size beds and electric blankets; water tower rooms have private baths with shower or tub/shower, one room in main house shares bath with tub/shower; no telephones; no television. Rates: moderate to expensive, breakfast included. No children. No pets. Cards: AE, MC, VISA. Open all year.

Getting There: From the south, when you reach the plaza, turn right.

Victorian Garden Inn

NAPA VALLEY

This lovely long valley, caressed by gentle mountains, is one of the world's most important winemaking regions. The Franciscan fathers from nearby Sonoma Mission started making wine here in the 1820s, but it was an inferior wine made from their Mission grapes. It was not until some thirty years later, in 1858, that Charles Krug produced the first European-type wine for which the valley is now known. After Colonel Agoston Haraszthy proved that the European *vinifera* grapes would thrive north of San Francisco Bay in his Buena Vista vineyards in Sonoma, French, Italian and German immigrants flocked to the Napa Valley in the 1860s, planting cuttings from Haraszthy's stock.

This viniferous valley stretches north from the city of Napa, an early timber-shipping center and once even a mining town during a silver rush in 1858. The valley ends at the town of Calistoga, whose mineral spas have attracted the weary since Mormon settler Sam Brannan first discovered underground hot springs here in 1859. Towering above Calistoga is the forty-five-hundred-foot peak of Mount St. Helena, which Robert Louis Stevenson described as the "Mont Blanc of the Coast Range" after spending his honeymoon in a bunkhouse at the mountain's base in 1880.

One of the most interesting settlements in the valley is Yountville, named after the valley's first white settler, George Yount. In exchange for a favor to his friend, General Vallejo, the Mexican government granted Yount an eleven-thousand-acre tract of land comprising most of the Napa Valley. The old Groezinger Winery in Yountville has been converted to a fascinating complex of shops, galleries and restaurants called Vintage 1870. Next door the train depot and railroad cars house yet more shops. And along the town's picturesque streets there are antique shops, restaurants—and a growing number of country inns.

North of Yountville is Rutherford Square, where outdoor musical productions are presented in the summer months. Just north of here is St. Helena, where a museum containing Robert Louis Stevenson memorabilia is housed in the town's library. Beyond the town are an old gristmill with a waterwheel forty feet in diameter, and Freemark Abbey, another interesting complex of shops.

Scattered throughout the valley and nestled in the surrounding hillsides are some one hundred and fifty wineries, most of which conduct tours of their cellars and tastings of their bottlings. This is unquestionably the most popular form of recreation in the valley. Space does not permit a description of all the wineries, but one stands out as spectacular over all the others. This is Sterling Vineyards, a Moorish-style structure on a hilltop in the center of the valley between St. Helena and Calistoga. An aerial tramway whisks visitors to the winery over treetops. Inside, the winemaking operation is explained graphically, allowing visitors to tour the premises at their own pace. Afterwards, sipping wine in the late afternoon on the terrace as the mountains cast their shadows onto the vineyards below is an experience long remembered.

Other forms of recreation in the Napa Valley include aerial gliding and ballooning around Calistoga, and swimming, fishing and boating at nearby Lake Berryessa. The valley also offers some of the finest dining in California. The cuisine is most often French nouvelle or Californian, but other ethnic styles are included, too.

Getting There: From San Francisco take Highway 101 north through San Rafael to Ignacio; there take Highway 37 east to Highway 21 north to the intersection of Highway 12 which leads east to Napa. From Napa Highway 29 extends north through Yountville, Rutherford and St. Helena to Calistoga.

Country Elegance in a Historic House
LA RESIDENCE
Napa

One of Napa Valley's early settlers was Harry C. Parker, a New Orleans river pilot who came to California during the 1849 gold rush. After working as a merchant in San Francisco and Stockton, he took up farming in Napa and in 1870 built himself a handsome three-story house just north of town. This is no ordinary farmhouse. It is built in the Gothic Revival style, with a columned porch and balcony onto which the large front bedrooms open. Marble or brick fireplaces enhance many of the rooms.

In 1981 Barbara Littenberg transformed the historic house into a charming inn and a few years later built a two-story structure next door. Topped with cupolas and sheathed with rustic shingles, the new unit looks like a barn that has been there forever. Inside, however, you will find luxurious amenities such as fireplaces, sitting areas and private baths. And though the rooms are new, they have an old-fashioned English country look with pine and oak furnishings and Laura Ashley prints. Most importantly, since the inn is located near Highway 29, the soundproofing keeps the rooms quiet as the countryside.

175

A light breakfast of fresh fruits, juices and house-baked breads, strudels or coffeecakes is served in the spacious dining room, warmed by a fire in nippy weather. French doors lead to the rear gardens and patio, where you will find a hot tub and Jacuzzi. At this writing new owners, David Jackson and Craig Claussen, have just taken over the inn and hope to add a swimming pool as well. They also plan an extensive remodeling of the original old house, which they intend to furnish with period antiques and rename The Mansion.

LA RESIDENCE, 4066 St. Helena Highway North (Highway 29), Napa, California 94558. Telephone: (707) 253-0337. Accommodations: twenty rooms with queen-size beds; most have private baths with tub/shower or stall shower; no telephones; no television. Rates: moderate to expensive, Continental breakfast included. No children. No pets. Cards: MC, VISA. Open all year.

Getting There: Take Highway 29 beyond Napa and past Salvador Road; turn right at Bon Appetit Restaurant, where a sign will direct you to the inn, which faces the highway.

True to its Vintage
MAGNOLIA HOTEL
Yountville

Built in 1873 with large stones from the Silverado Trail, this small three-story hotel has had a checkered history. Originally a traveler paid a dollar a night for a room, including a barn and feed for his horse. Those who could afford the luxury of rail travel were met at the Yountville depot by a surrey sent by the hotel. At one time the Magnolia was reputedly a brothel, and it is known fact that the cellar was a center for bootlegging activities during Prohibition. Then the hotel was boarded up for many years, until Ray and Nancy Monte purchased it in 1968 and restored it to an inn of eminent charm and respectability. In 1977 the Magnolia was again sold, to Bruce Locken, former general manager of the Clift Hotel in San Francisco, and his wife Bonnie. They have continued the improvement process, adding four luxurious new rooms with decks and fireplaces in an adjoining building, and refurbishing an old carriage house.

Furnishings are from the Victorian era: marble-topped tables with crystal decanters of port in the bedrooms, antique brass or wooden

Magnolia Hotel

bedsteads with crocheted or quilted spreads, and everywhere dozens of handmade dolls and pillows that Bonnie has collected over the years. Concessions to twentieth-century living have been made, however, with private tiled baths throughout. Many of the rooms have splendid views of the vineyards across the road.

Breakfast here, announced by the ringing of a gong at precisely nine o'clock, is an important event at the Magnolia. Guests gather in the restaurant adjoining the hotel, introduce themselves and share wine-touring tips. Bruce, a skilled raconteur, moves around the table, telling anecdotes from several decades of hotel keeping while replenishing the coffeepot and serving generous platters of food. The Lockens' system of devising the menu is unique: First-nighters are served french toast with port-wine syrup, second-nighters get shirred eggs, third-nighters receive a sherry and mushroom omelet, and so on, so that no one has the same breakfast two mornings in a row.

After a day of winery touring, you can relax in the large swimming pool surrounded by lawns. Here—or in your room if you like—Bruce will serve you a bottle purchased from his fine collection of Napa wines. And behind the hotel, set in an enclosed redwood deck, is a commodious Jacuzzi pool, which is lighted from under the water at night.

MAGNOLIA HOTEL, 6529 Yount Street, Yountville, California 94599. Telephone: (707) 944-2056. Accommodations: twelve rooms with double, queen- and king-size beds; private baths with shower only; no telephones; no television. Rates: moderate to very expensive, breakfast included. No children under 16. No pets. No credit cards. No smoking. Open all year.

Spectacular Views of the Valley

AUBERGE DU SOLEIL
Rutherford

The original concept was to create a French country inn amid the olive groves on a hillside above the Napa Valley. Somewhere along the way, a southwestern motif was introduced, resulting in a wine-country retreat that is uniquely Californian with stunning panoramic views of the lush vineyards below.

And *every* room does have a view and a deck, outfitted with chaises from which to admire the vista. In fact, you might just want to spend the whole day here, starting with a breakfast tray of orange juice, coffee, croissants, bran muffins and the morning paper. Help yourself to some fruit from the well-stocked wet bar, where you will also find pâté, cheese, wine, champagne, beer and liquors for toasting the sunset. (The fruit and breakfast are complimentary; there's an "honor-bar" charge for the other goodies.) And on those rare days when the sun doesn't shine at the "Inn of the Sun," you can build a cheery fire at the handsome hearth, faced with Spanish tile. Even taking a bath here is special, under a skylight in a tub for two.

The guest accommodations are located in nine buildings of four units each, terraced up the hillside. A pool and tennis courts are nearby. And sited above it all are the inn itself and its renowned restaurant, which made international culinary headlines when the late, great Masa Kobayashi was the chef here.

AUBERGE DU SOLEIL, 180 Rutherford Hill Road, Rutherford, California 94573. Telephone: (707) 963-1211. Accommodations: eighteen rooms and eighteen suites with twin and king-size beds; private baths with tubs and showers; one room fully equipped for handicapped; telephones; color television. Rates: extremely expensive. Continental breakfast included. Children welcome. Pets permitted with deposit. Cards: MC, VISA. Open all year.

Getting There: From Napa, take the Silverado Trail north to Rutherford Hill Road. From Rutherford, take Highway 128 east to the Silverado Trail and turn left.

New Life for a Century-Old Hotel

HOTEL ST. HELENA

St. Helena

In 1881, while the Beringers and Krugs were busy expanding their wineries, an elegant two-story hotel opened on St. Helena's Main Street. But as the wineries flourished, the hotel deteriorated, its rooms eventually little better than those of flophouses, its lower floor occupied by a branch of Montgomery Ward. Almost a century later Santa Barbara developer Carl Johnson bought the hotel and restored it to a degree of luxury it had probably never known before.

You enter through a flower-filled arcade to the lobby and a cozy wine bar. Here and on an adjoining patio a complimentary breakfast of juice, fruit, croissants and muffins is served. Upstairs, a lounge and eighteen guest rooms have been skillfully decorated by Tom Brooks and Linda Daniels, who combined antiques with modern comforts. The hall is papered with a striped and floral pattern of burgundy, tan and brown— setting the color scheme for all the rooms. In the sitting room at the top of the stairs, love seats upholstered in burgundy velvet flank a fireplace.

The bedrooms are painted in colors of burgundy, mauve, chocolate brown, dark tan or pale gold; patterned quilted bedspreads and dust ruffles echo these hues. The larger rooms have headboards of brass or carved wood, armoires, lounge chairs and round, cloth-covered tables. The smaller rooms have painted iron headboards and ladderback chairs. Four rooms without private baths have bent-willow headboards and marble-topped commodes with baskets of fresh towels and soap. There's also a suite with a sitting room. All the rooms are richly carpeted; windows are shuttered in white throughout. At the rear of the hotel, overlooking the arcade, is a wide deck with chaises and tables: a restful spot to relax before or after a day of winery touring.

HOTEL ST. HELENA, 1309 Main Street (Highway 29), St. Helena, California 94574. Telephone: (707) 963-4388. Accommodations: eighteen rooms with twin or queen-size beds; fourteen rooms have private baths with stall shower or tub/shower; four rooms share two baths; no telephones; no television. Rates: moderate to expensive, Continental breakfast included. No children. No pets. Cards: AE, MC, VISA. Open all year.

1881

HOTEL ST. HELENA

Hotel St. Helena

A Dream Come True
WINE COUNTRY INN
St. Helena

Though constructed in 1975, the Wine Country Inn is one of the oldest, continuously operated wine-country hostelries in this book. That shows how recent is the inn boom in the Napa Valley. Ned and Marge Smith had long dreamed of opening an inn, and for several years they spent vacations touring the inns of New England to get ideas and advice. One warning they heeded: "Don't restore an old building, build a new one. There will be fewer headaches and more comforts." The Wine Country Inn, nevertheless, looks as though it has been sitting on its hillock surrounded by vineyards forever. That's the way the owners wanted it to look. The three-story structure of stone and wood with dormered windows and a gabled tower represents a composite of ideas borrowed from historic buildings in the valley. Several years later the Smiths added two smaller buildings nearby, and recently put in a pool and spa.

Comfort is the key word here. All rooms are carpeted and have modern baths. The furnishings are antique, from a potpourri of periods, but the old four-poster beds have been widened to queen size and the brass-framed doubles elongated. The rooms are papered with a floral motif and each is different, but romantic in its own way. Fifteen of the rooms have freestanding fireplaces, seven have patios landscaped for privacy, and twelve have intimate balconies. Some have window seats in alcoves with views of the surrounding countryside.

On the ground floor of the main building is a large, homey common room, equipped with card tables and books on wine. Here in the mornings, at a long refectory table, a Continental breakfast is served of fresh fruits and juices, assorted hot breads and coffee. On warmer days this repast is served on a deck outside.

WINE COUNTRY INN, 1152 Lodi Lane, St. Helena, California 94574. Telephone: (707) 963-7077. Accommodations: twenty-five rooms with twin, double or queen-size beds; private baths, some with tub/shower, some shower only, seven rooms with wheelchair access; no telephones; no television. Rates: expensive to very expensive. Continental breakfast included. No children under 12. No pets. Cards: MC, VISA. Open all year.

Getting There: From Napa take Highway 29 two miles past St. Helena and turn right on Lodi Lane.

Wine Country Inn

Where Pines Replace the Vines
MEADOWOOD
St. Helena

The mountains east of St. Helena rise from the vineyards to embrace a small, secluded canyon studded with pines. This sylvan vale shelters the Meadowood Resort, a complex of lodges and cottages scattered over a 256-acre reserve—secluded on the wooded hillsides, or overlooking the golf course or the pool or the tennis and croquet courts. Meadowood was originally a private club, conceived as a playground for local vintners, but in the mid-1980s (after the original clubhouse burned to the ground), the complex was rebuilt as a luxurious resort and conference center.

From the outside, the fourplex lodges that house the accommodations look rustic and old-fashioned. Inside, the suites and bedrooms are modern as tomorrow—many with skylights set in pitched ceilings, comfortable sitting areas, fireplaces of Silverado stone, and wet bars abundantly stocked with wine, beer, soft drinks and fruit. (It's replenished daily and added to your bill.) Meadowood pampers. No less than six pillows are heaped on the quilt-covered, king-size beds. White terrycloth robes hang in the closets. And a phone call will bring a masseuse.

Meadowood's Starmont Restaurant, with its view of the golf course and hills, offers some of the best food in the Napa Valley, the work of Hawaiian-born Hale Lake, who has developed his own style of contemporary California cooking. The resort also serves as headquarters for the Napa Valley Vintners Association and the Napa Valley Wine Auction, so it is no surprise that it has one of the best selections of California bottlings in the state.

MEADOWOOD RESORT, 900 Meadowood Lane, St. Helena, California 94574. Telephone: (707) 963-3646, in California (800) 458-8080. Accommodations: fifty-one studios or suites with king-size beds, some also with Murphy beds or fold-out beds; private baths with tub/shower or stall shower; some rooms handicap accessible; telephones; television. Rates: expensive to very expensive, no meals included. Open to the public for lunch and dinner; full bar service. Children welcome. No pets. Cards: AE, MC, VISA. Open all year.

Getting There: From Napa take Silverado Trail north to Howell Mountain Road, turn right and follow signs to Meadowood. From St. Helena go east on Pope Street, which becomes Howell Mountain Road.

LARKMEAD COUNTRY INN
Calistoga

Lillie Coit is best known for her devotion to San Francisco's firemen and for the monument she had built for them on Telegraph Hill: Coit Tower. Few people connect her with wine history, but she owned the Larkmead Vineyards south of Calistoga in the 1880s. A later owner was Swiss-born Felix Salmina, who in 1918 built for his son and daughter-in-law a sprawling clapboard Victorian in the middle of his vineyards. The Hans Kornell winery, whose champagne cellars are next door, now owns the grape lands. Gene and Joan Garbarino bought the lovely old house for a second residence and then decided in 1979 to run it as a country inn.

Through fieldstone gates the driveway leads to a wisteria-covered loggia in the rear of the house. Up some stairs is the gracious living room appointed with a Persian carpet, antiques that the Garbarinos have collected in their European travels and a well-stocked library. A fire burns on the hearth evenings and mornings when guests gather for breakfast in the adjoining dining room. The table, which seats ten, is elegantly set with sterling silver and peony-patterned porcelain plates on which Joan artfully arranges grapes and slices of watermelon, oranges, pears, peaches, kiwis—whatever is in season. Then individual baskets of croissants, scones and french rolls are served with crocks of sweet butter.

European etchings and oil paintings grace the dining and living rooms, as well as the four bedrooms. These are named after various wines and command spectacular views of the vineyards. Chablis, dressed up in muted green tones, features an enclosed sun porch off the bedroom, while Beaujolais has private use of the open porch over the loggia. Chenin Blanc is feminine and flowery with draperies, wallpaper and a chaise covered in matching patterns. And Chardonnay has an art deco look, with old brass bedsteads that came from a Parisian hotel. Fresh flowers are placed in all the rooms.

The Larkmead Inn is surrounded by wide verandas and lawns shaded by sycamores, magnolias and cypress. It's a peaceful haven you will be reluctant to leave. But you don't have to go far for wine touring. Just walk next door to the winery, where Hans Kornell himself or members of his family will explain in detail the process of making bottle-fermented champagnes.

LARKMEAD COUNTRY INN, 1103 Larkmead Lane, Calistoga, California 94515. Telephone: (707) 942-5360. Accommodations: four rooms with twin or double beds; private baths with stall showers; air conditioning; no telephones; no television. Rates: expensive. Continental breakfast included. No children. No pets. No credit cards. Open all year.

Getting There: Take Highway 29, and north of St. Helena turn right on Larkmead Lane.

A Small, Homey Place
WINE WAY INN
Calistoga

Once a sleepy, slightly run-down resort town, Calistoga is now a lively community with restored hotels, shops and restaurants lining its quaint main street. On the edge of town, at the base of a forested mountainside, is the Wine Way Inn. Built in 1915 as a private residence, the small house still retains a homey feeling, reinforced by the warm hospitality of innkeepers Allen and Dede Good, who have owned the place since 1980. Refreshments are offered to newly arrived guests, who can sit and unwind on the huge overstuffed couch in front of the fireplace in the fir-paneled living room-dining area. The rear wall here is entirely covered with cupboards, their leaded glass doors revealing a fine collection of silver, china and pewter. Round breakfast tables are covered with brown and blue checkered cloths and blue underskirts and surrounded by ladderback chairs. Café curtains are at the windows. The morning meal—a choice of three or four breads and pastries, plus orange juice and fruit—is served here or on the immense deck behind the house. Furnished with picnic tables and chaises, this is a great place to relax and stare at the mountain above. Now covered with redwoods and maples, the terraced slopes were once vineyards, the second oldest in the area.

Upstairs, the five bedrooms are small and pretty with gabled ceilings, antiques, and beds covered with heirloom patchwork quilts that range in age from seventy-five to a hundred years. In the rear a tiny cottage, once a carriage house, with half-timbered walls and a private porch, nestles among the trees.

WINE WAY INN, 1019 Foothill Boulevard (Highway 29), Calistoga, California 94515. Telephone: (707) 942-0680. Accommodations: five rooms with double or queen-size beds; three rooms and cottage have private baths with stall shower; two rooms share bath with tub/shower; no telephones; no television; air conditioned. Rates: moderate, Continental breakfast included. No children under 10. No pets. Smoking discouraged in bedrooms. Cards: MC, VISA. Open all year.

Vineyards to Rival Nearby Napa
RUSSIAN RIVER VALLEY
From Cloverdale to Guerneville

From its origin in Mendocino County, the Russian River winds over two hundred miles through the lush vineyards of northern Sonoma County and through the redwood-forested coastal mountains to the Pacific. The first settlers here engaged in agriculture and lumber, but in the last quarter of the nineteenth century vineyards began to appear, from Guerneville in the south, where the Korbel cellars were established in 1886, to Cloverdale in the north, home of Italian Swiss Colony since 1887. Until very recently, however, most of the other wineries in this region produced mostly inexpensive wines. Then in the late 1960s, at the peak of California's wine boom, winemakers began to realize that the climate and soil of this area were capable of producing premium grapes to rival those of nearby Napa—particularly in the Alexander and Dry Creek valleys. Today twenty-seven wineries are bottling varietal wines from the vineyards alongside the Russian River, among them such prestigious names as Davis Bynum, Simi, Trentadue and Dry Creek. Many have tasting rooms, winery tours, and picnic areas. (Specific information on these wineries, a map showing their locations, and schedules of forthcoming special events such as fairs, musicals, art shows and barrel tastings can be obtained from The Russian River Wine Road, P.O. Box 127, Geyserville, California 95441.) The advent of the premium grape in the Russian River Valley was followed inevitably by the appearance of country inns in the river towns from Cloverdale to Guerneville.

Getting There: From San Francisco, Highway 101 passes through Healdsburg, Geyserville and Cloverdale. Guerneville is reached by taking River Road west, just north of Santa Rosa. From the Napa Valley, Highway 29 leads from Calistoga to Geyserville.

Triple-Towered Queen Anne

VINTAGE TOWERS

Cloverdale

This turn-of-the-century Queen Anne has not one but *three* towers—one round, one square and one octagonal. The stately old mansion was converted into an inn in 1980 and is now owned by Dan and Lauri Weddle. The tower suites are the choicest of the inn's charming guest rooms, with sitting areas in the turrets; one has a private balcony. But even the least expensive room here is attractive—a bright, cozy sun porch with windows on three sides.

The spacious downstairs rooms promise a paradise for readers, with a collection of one thousand books. But music lovers will be happy here too. There are a piano and a "piano player," a device that is set on the keyboard to bang out tunes from a large collection of player-piano rolls. Nearby an old-fashioned Victrola is stocked with several hundred records.

The wood-paneled dining room has a fireplace and windows looking out to the lawn and rose gardens. Dan is the cook in the family and fixes hearty breakfasts of juice, fruit and interesting entrées that change daily: chili-cheese egg puff served with fresh apple bread, french toast with raspberry sauce and bacon, and ricotta-cheese pancakes topped with blueberries and sour cream are but a few of the possibilities. On nice mornings guests may breakfast on the wide veranda, where refreshments are also served on balmy evenings. And set in the gardens is a gazebo, which is a popular site for weddings.

Vintage Towers provides bicycles for exploring the town and countryside. There are, of course, many wineries in the area. And only minutes away you will find swimming, canoeing and tubing in the Russian River, and boating, fishing and waterskiing in the newly opened Lake Sonoma.

VINTAGE TOWERS, 302 North Main Street, Cloverdale, California 95425. Telephone: (707) 894-4535. Accommodations: eight rooms with double, queen- or king-size beds; six rooms with private baths, two share one bath, tub or tub/shower; no telephones; no television; air conditioning. Rates: inexpensive to moderate, breakfast included. No children under 10. No pets. No smoking. Cards: MC, VISA. Facilities for weddings and small conferences. Open all year.

Getting There: From San Francisco take Highway 101 north to the first stop light in Cloverdale; turn right for one block; then turn left on Main.

In Celebration of Victoriana

HOPE-MERRILL HOUSE
HOPE-BOSWORTH HOUSE
Geyserville

In the sleepy town of Geyserville, Bob and Rosalie Hope offer an escape back to the nineteenth century in two authentically restored Victorian houses and a trek through the vineyards in an 1882 stagecoach. Before moving to Geyserville in 1980, the Hopes had operated a resort farther down the Russian River, while Rosalie pursued with a passion her hobby of collecting Victoriana. This assemblage of period furniture and bric-a-brac formed the nucleus for decorating their present inn complex.

Their first project was a 1904 Queen Anne cottage built from a pattern book by the Bosworth family, pioneers of the area. Rechristened Hope-Bosworth, the inn is papered with reproductions of Victorian wall coverings, but the furnishings in the cozy parlor, dining room and four upstairs bedrooms are genuine antiques from the era. A rear sun porch opens to a pretty garden with a grape arbor.

The Hope-Merrill House is a stately century-old Eastlake-Stick that stands on land once occupied by the Geyserville Hotel, which was a Wells Fargo stage stop. Here the wallpapers are magnificent custom-made replicas of *fin de siècle* patterns, complete with a frieze around the ceilings. The hall wainscoting is an original Lincrusta Walton pattern, unpainted and in mint condition. The pride of the high-ceilinged formal sitting room is a five-piece Eastlake walnut parlor set, with chairs upholstered in cranberry velvet. Pieces of cranberry glass, cut glass and crystal embellish the room. The dining room is distinguished by Tudor-style furnishings and a massive 1871 cast-iron chandelier with its original shades.

But back to those stagecoach rides. On weekends from May through October, the Hopes cosponsor "Stage-A-Picnic" for their guests and others. The old stage, drawn by teams of Belgian draft horses, rambles through the vineyards for several hours, stopping at small wineries for a tipple along the way. The tour concludes at the grape arbor of Trentadue Winery for a grand picnic featuring the famed cheeses, sausage and produce of Sonoma.

After lunch it's back to the inn for a dip in the Hopes' new pool or a nap in one of the cozy bedrooms, where visions of vineyards peek through lace-curtained windows. Some of these rooms also contain pieces of museum quality, such as an 1865 walnut and burl headboard and an 1850 child's crib. And if you need some reading material, you're likely to find on the bedside table some gems from Rosalie's collection of Victorian-era books.

Homemade preserves and breads with fruit and juice start the day at both Hope houses. Refreshments are offered in the evening. With advance notice and a minimum party of six, the Hopes will also prepare catered dinners at either of the houses. But you need not worry about going hungry in Geyserville. Just down the road is Catelli's, a bastion of home-cooked, old-style Italian food. And nearby the Souverain Winery runs a beautiful restaurant set in the midst of their vineyards.

HOPE-MERRILL HOUSE, 21253 Geyserville Avenue, Geyserville, California 95441. Telephone: (707) 857-3356. Accommodations: five rooms with double or queen-size beds; three rooms have private baths with shower or tub/shower and two rooms share a bath; no telephones; no television. Rates: moderate, breakfast included. No pets. No smoking. Cards: MC, VISA. Open all year.

HOPE-BOSWORTH HOUSE, 21238 Geyserville Avenue, Geyserville, California 95441. Telephone: (707) 857-3356. Accommodations: five rooms with double or queen-size beds; private and shared baths; no telephones; no television. Rates: moderate, breakfast included. No pets. No smoking. Cards: MC, VISA. Open all year.

STAGE-A-PICNIC Advance reservations must be made by calling (707) 857-3619; they may also be made by calling the inn. The morning tour departs at ten o'clock; an afternoon tour is preceded by the picnic lunch, which starts at 12:30. The charge, at this writing, is $35 per person.

Hope-Merrill House

A Nabob's Palatial Country Home

MADRONA MANOR
Healdsburg

In 1881 one of San Francisco's nabobs, financier John Paxton, spared no costs to build a three-story mansion with a gabled mansard roof on a wooded knoll overlooking the Russian River valley. Even though the manor was only to be a summer home, he lavished it with fourteen-foot-high ceilings, ten fireplaces inlaid with brightly painted tiles, and floors of Italian mosaic, and furnished it with massive pieces of carved walnut and mahogany.

When Carol and John Muir (a distant cousin of the naturalist) discovered this country estate a century later, they knew it was the perfect site for the inn they had been dreaming of when John had served as a Bechtel executive in Saudi Arabia. Although the mansion needed a lot of repair, the original furnishings were still in place and the Muirs added only the fine Persian carpets they had acquired in their travels. On the lower floors of the mansion, five guest rooms, each with fireplace and private bath, contain hundred-year-old, ten-foot-high four-posters or carved headboards, gigantic armoires and marble-topped dressers. You almost feel like you are sleeping in a museum. The third floor shelters four cozy little rooms under the eaves.

Behind his mansion Paxton had built a carpenter gothic carriage house. The Muirs reconstructed its interior, which holds a large common room with fireplace and game tables, along with eight guest rooms furnished with carved rosewood tables and chairs that they had commissioned in Nepal for their then nonexistent dream inn. Although the carriage house rooms—with twin or queen-size beds and modern baths—are undoubtedly more comfortable than those in the main house, they lack the opulent style of the manor rooms. Two other outbuildings have been remodeled as two-room suites, each with its own sitting room.

Yet the sleeping accommodations are only half the story of Madrona Manor. The food reaches a quality that even Paxton, with all his millions, probably never enjoyed. The dining rooms and kitchen are the domain of the Muirs' son Todd and his sous-chef Mark Holmoe, both graduates of San Francisco's Culinary Academy. Their cooking is in the California, or more specifically Sonoma, style, utilizing the seasonal bounties of the county. Breakfast consists of fresh fruits, platters of smoked meats and local cheeses, soft-boiled eggs, toast and *churros* (little deep-fried pastries), served with house-made apricot and

The Carriage House at Madrona Manor

kiwi jam. The restaurant is open to the public for dinner and features unusual pastas, smoked salmon, trout and duck from the manor's own smokehouse, and mesquite-grilled meats, poultry and seafood. A Sunday brunch is served on the terrace, when weather permits.

Madrona Manor sits on eight acres of orchards and gardens studded with oaks, redwoods and the palms that Paxton planted a century ago. But the Muirs have added one luxury that the nabob never dreamed of—a swimming pool.

MADRONA MANOR, 1001 Westside Road (Box 818), Healdsburg, California 95448. Telephone: (707) 433-4231. Accommodations: eighteen rooms and two suites with twin, double, queen- or king-size beds; private baths with tub/shower; no television; no telephones. Rates: expensive, full breakfast included. Restaurant open for dinner and Sunday brunch. Children and pets welcome. Cards: AE, MC, VISA. Open all year.

Getting There: From San Francisco take second Healdsburg exit off Highway 101 and follow Healdsburg Avenue north to Mill Road which becomes Westside Road. From the north take Westside Road exit from Highway 101.

Even the Nuns Return
THE HAYDON HOUSE
Healdsburg

This 1912 Queen Anne on a quiet side street of Healdsburg exudes the warmth and charm of a well-run country home. You would never guess that three decades of housing a convent, then a boys' home and eventually a rest home had taken their toll on the place. But innkeepers Joanne and Richard Claus painstakingly removed the traces of institutional wear and tear, including the asphalt tiles that covered all the floors. Now the gleaming natural fir contrasts splendidly with pastel Dhurrie rugs, handmade in India. The five second-floor bedrooms are decorated with French and American antiques, custom-made down quilts that match the bed linens, baskets of mixed dried and silk flowers and Laura Ashley prints. Only one room presently has a private bath, but the others have washstands set in old-fashioned dressers and three have claw-legged tubs with ring showers in the room. The *pièce de résistance* of the Haydon House restoration is a former attic space over the porch, now brightly illuminated by skylights in the sloping roof. Two additional rooms with private baths are scheduled to open in 1987.

Joanne is particularly proud of her buffet breakfasts, served in the large, sunny dining room off the comfortable double parlor. She changes the menu, but a typical repast includes freshly squeezed orange juice, fresh pineapple and a compote of seasonal fruits, two frittatas (one meatless and one with sausage), a freshly baked coffee-cake and apple, bran or blueberry muffins. A lot of guests return just for the breakfasts. But Haydon House itself is a place people want to come back to. Even the nuns from the convent drop in to see their former home.

HAYDON HOUSE, 321 Haydon Street, Healdsburg, California 95448. Telephone: (707) 433-5228. Accommodations: five rooms with double or queen-size beds, additional sofa bed in attic room; one private bath, three rooms with tub/showers in rooms, one room with private shower across hall, one and one-half community baths; no telephones; color television in parlor. Rates: moderate, breakfast included. No children under 13. No pets. No smoking in guest rooms. Cards: MC, VISA. Open all year.

Getting There: From Highway 101 take second Healdsburg exit to the plaza, turn right on Matheson. Drive three blocks to Fitch and turn right. Drive another two blocks to Haydon and turn left.

THE GRAPE LEAF INN
Healdsburg

In the heart of the Russian River wine country is the quiet town of Healdsburg, its side streets lined with trees and Victorian houses, many of which have been turned into inns in recent years. One of the first to offer bed and breakfast was the Grape Leaf Inn, a 1901 Victorian that was converted by airline stewardess Laura Salo and furnished with antiques she had collected in her travels—Austrian headboards, Oriental rugs, brass coat stands.

Real estate broker Terry Sweet bought the inn and furnishings and added another four luxurious units to the previously unused second floor. These have stained-glass dormer windows and skylights set in the pitched roof, private baths with Jacuzzi tubs and full air conditioning. The lower floor now contains three bedrooms and a large double parlor with a fireplace, lots of books and a dining table by the café-curtained windows. You may breakfast here or in a cheerful alcove off the country kitchen. And it is a real breakfast too, with eggs, fresh ground coffees and home-baked breads. In the afternoon, wines from Sonoma County are served in the parlor or out on the wide veranda that shades two sides of the house and overlooks the pretty garden.

GRAPE LEAF INN, 539 Johnson Street, Healdsburg, California 95448. Telephone: (707) 433-8140. Accommodations: seven rooms with queen- or king-size beds; private baths, some with whirlpool, tub/showers for two; no telephones; no television. Rates: moderate to expensive, full breakfast included. No children. No pets. No smoking. Cards: MC, VISA. Open all year.

Getting There: From Highway 101 take Headsburg Avenue exit to Grant and turn right. Drive two blocks to Johnson.

A Touch of France in Sonoma County
VINTNERS INN
Santa Rosa

Ex-New Yorker John Duffy is a nuclear physicist. His wife Francisca is a European-born trilingual interpreter and former Pan American flight attendant. How did this couple wind up as vineyardists and innkeepers in Sonoma County? It started in the mid-1970s, when they began to seek "the ultimate lifestyle" and bought a century-old, fifty-acre prune ranch four miles north of Santa Rosa. After replanting the fields with premium grapes, they decided to build, among their vineyards, an inn inspired by the villages of Provence.

In 1984 the luxurious Vintners Inn was completed. Four stucco buildings with pitched red-tile roofs cluster around a plaza complete with bubbling fountain and French streetlights. The interiors, designed by Francisca, have an elegant, understated French-country aura with delicate multifloral wallpapers and woven cotton prints. Except for the

custom-made beds, the furnishings are European pine antiques, all authentic, as are the old farm implements scattered throughout the inn. The guest rooms have beamed ceilings, comfortable seating areas and french doors opening to balconies or patios; some have wood-burning fireplaces. In each room an armoire conceals a color television, and portable VCRs are available for viewing films, old and new, from the Duffy's large collection.

So, you're not a movie buff; well, the handsome library in the main building is well stocked with books and games. But on balmy days, you'll be tempted outside by the twelve-foot spa and its surrounding sundeck on the edge of the vineyard. And if you're looking for more strenuous recreation, inn guests have swimming, golfing and tennis privileges at a nearby country club. At certain times of the year the Duffys also organize "Art in the Wine Country" weekends with seminars and tours of local galleries. There are murder mystery weekends, too, when you can be the sleuth—or even the suspect.

As in Provence, food plays an important role at Vintners Inn. In the pretty tile-floored dining room, you can help yourself from a bountiful breakfast buffet of fruits, jams, croissants, cereals; there is even a waffle iron to make your own. In the afternoon and evening, light snacks are available through room service. And at this writing, construction is underway on a fifth building in the inn complex to house the restaurant of John Ash, one of America's most talented and highly acclaimed young chefs.

Vintners Inn has one drawback: it's near the freeway. Request a room facing the vineyards.

VINTNERS INN, 4350 Barnes Road, Santa Rosa, California 95401. Telephone: (800) 421-2584, California only; (707) 575-7350. Accommodations: forty-four rooms with queen-size beds; private baths with tub and shower; some rooms fully equipped for handicapped; telephones; television. Rates: high moderate to expensive, breakfast included. Children and pets welcome. Cards: AE, CB, DC, MC, VISA. Facilities for weddings and small conferences. Open all year.

Getting There: From San Francisco take Highway 101 north past Santa Rosa to River Road/Guerneville exit. Barnes Road is the first road just after you cross back over the freeway. Turn left.

RIDENHOUR RANCH HOUSE INN

Guerneville

As the Russian River nears Guerneville, its valley narrows and the redwoods become denser. Here, next to the Korbel vineyards, is another old ranch house restored as a charming inn. It dates back to 1856, when Louis William Ridenhour began to farm 940 acres of the fertile lands on both sides of the river. In 1906 his son, Louis E. Ridenhour, built his home of heart redwood on several acres of the ranch. In 1977 Martha and Bob Satterthwaite bought the house and created a gracious hostelry with the ambience of a private home, a quiet haven well away from the honky-tonk river resorts.

Fireplaces, Oriental rugs, comfortable furnishings and a profusion of greenery and African violets grace the large redwood-paneled living room and adjoining dining room. You can breakfast here, or in the cheerful family kitchen, or out on the patio—a light repast of freshly ground coffee, teas, nut breads or muffins, fresh juices, fruits (sometimes from the inn's own gardens) and a variety of cheeses. The two spacious downstairs bedrooms have queen-size beds with Victorian headboards and quilted spreads; each of these has a private bath, and one has a little sitting room with a couch that folds into a bed. Upstairs three cozy little rooms with dormer windows nestle under the eaves, sharing a bath. These have an Early American look with hooked rugs and chenille

spreads or handmade quilts. Fresh flowers, plants and the original touches of Martha Satterthwaite, a former interior designer, are here and there: straw hats on the wall of one room and on another a Japanese kite fashioned from calico fabric. Another two rooms with private entrances occupy a lower level, and recently an eighth room with its own fireplace has been added. Every room of this inn provides sylvan views of surrounding oaks and redwoods or the Korbel vineyards next door. A stroll through these woods and through the gardens informally landscaped with daisies, zinnias, and marigolds is a favorite pastime here. Other diversions include a redwood hot tub and a croquet court. The Korbel champagne cellars and secluded river beaches are a short walk away.

RIDENHOUR RANCH HOUSE, 12850 River Road, Guerneville, California 95446. Telephone: (707) 887-1033. Accommodations: eight rooms with queen-size, double or two double beds; five rooms with private baths with tub/shower; three rooms share bath with shower; no telephones; no television; wheelchair access to one room. Rates: moderate, breakfast included. Children over 10 welcome. No pets. Smoking permitted in living room only. Cards: MC, VISA. Open all year.

Getting There: From Highway 101 take River Road exit north of Santa Rosa and drive west twelve miles.

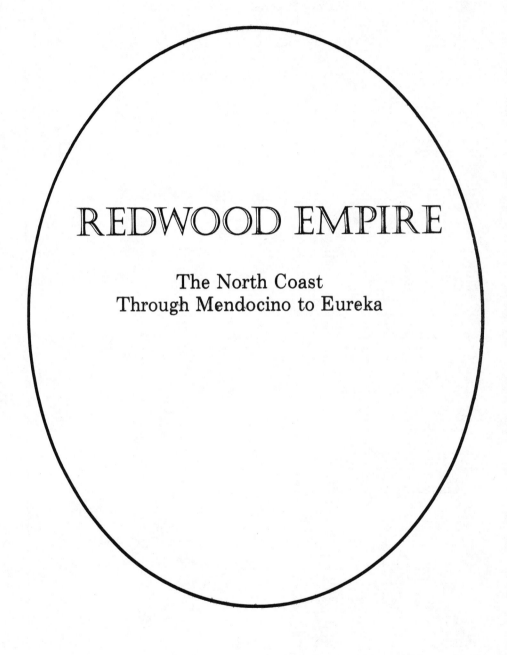

REDWOOD EMPIRE

The North Coast
Through Mendocino to Eureka

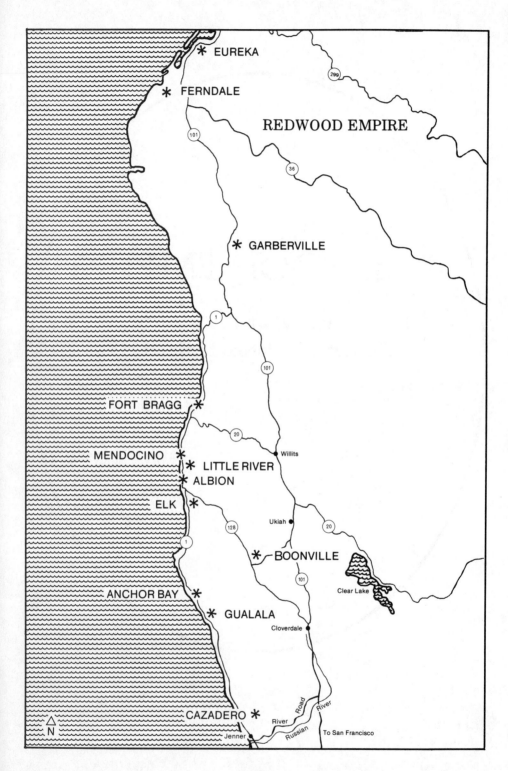

EUREKA

FERNDALE

REDWOOD EMPIRE

GARBERVILLE

FORT BRAGG

Willits

MENDOCINO
LITTLE RIVER
ALBION

ELK

Ukiah

128

20

BOONVILLE

101

Clear Lake

ANCHOR BAY

GUALALA

Cloverdale

CAZADERO

River

Road

River

River

Russian

To San Francisco

Jenner

N

202

Where Forested Mountains Meet the Sea
NORTH COAST

North of Jenner, where the Russian River meets the Pacific, Highway 1 soars upwards, switchbacking through mountainous terrain, then stretches north along the craggy coast to Mendocino. This awesome drive through mostly isolated countryside takes you past the reconstruction of Fort Ross, the site of a Russian seal- and otter-trapping settlement in the early 1800s. It also takes you past numerous coves where weathered pilings and abandoned cemeteries are the only testimony to the once-thriving lumber towns that studded the coast in the last century. From the forested mountains that rise from the sea, millions of redwood trees were hewn to build the Victorians of San Francisco.

Getting There: To reach Highway 1 from San Francisco, take Highway 101 north to Petaluma; take Washington Street exit to the road leading to Bodega Bay, then proceed north on Highway 1. An alternative route is Highway 116, north of Petaluma, west to Highway 1. For about ten miles north of Jenner this road winds along cliffs high above the ocean; it can be hazardous or closed in bad weather and it can frighten people who are bothered by heights. But this drive is breathtakingly beautiful, and the quickest route to Gualala (allow about three hours from San Francisco).

The shortest route to Mendocino, however, is the inland approach via Highway 128, which takes about three and one-half hours, as opposed to some five hours via Highway 1. Take 101 north to Cloverdale and Highway 128 west to the coast where it intercepts Highway 1 just south of Albion and north of Elk. The best way to tour the north coast is to drive up Highway 1 (you will feel safer because your car is on the inside of the road, away from the cliffs) and return via 128.

Enjoying the Great Outdoors in Style
TIMBERHILL RANCH
Timber Cove Ridge

Amid eighty acres of pines, redwoods and live oaks on a ridge eleven hundred feet above the Pacific, Timberhill Ranch provides an idyllic retreat for those who enjoy the great outdoors, yet like to live in style. The property is both an inn and a working ranch where horses, goats, rabbits and llamas are raised.

Timberhill is also the home of Barbara and Frank Watson and Tarran and Michael Riordan, who opened this unique vacation getaway in 1984. Doing most of the work themselves, they transformed an old ranch house into a splendid lodge with skylights in the pitched ceilings, stone fireplaces in the dining and living rooms and redwood decks. They also built ten guest cottages, spaced far apart among the trees, and added a lovely swimming pool, an outdoor Jacuzzi spa and two tennis courts.

A stay at Timberhill is designed so that you never have to leave the ranch. Included in the rate are three meals a day, prepared by professional chefs and not exactly your typical ranch food. A six-course dinner is served at candlelit tables for two, set with fresh flowers, family silver, china and crystal—even silver napkin rings. A typical menu starts with carpaccio, cream of broccoli soup, California waldorf salad and pink grapefruit sorbet. You have a choice of five entrées ranging from loin of lamb with garlic cream to mahimahi in coconut ginger-cream, and a selection of four or five sumptuous house-made pastries and desserts. If you're on a diet, however, Timberhill (with advance notice) will prepare a special menu: low-sodium, sugar-free, Pritikin or whatever.

Coffee is often served by the fire in the living room, where you can while away the evening at the chess board or with a jigsaw puzzle or a book from a library of leather-bound volumes. Flashlights are provided for the walk to your cottage, but often they're not needed, as the starlight in these mountains is inordinately bright.

Although the cabins look rustic from outside, the interiors are luxuriously appointed in a charming country style. Pitched ceilings and walls are sheathed with knotty cedar, glass doors open to a private deck, a wood fire is ready to light in the raised hearth and the bed is covered with a handmade patchwork quilt. Flowers are everywhere—in bouquets on the table, on the pillows of the turned-down bed; you'll even find blossoms tucked atop the towels and the toilet paper in the tiled bathroom.

In the morning many guests like to help feed the animals before breakfast, which is a full meal with all the trimmings, centering around crêpes, pancakes or eggs any style. Lunch (sometimes a buffet and sometimes a simple meal like lovash sandwiches, salad and soup) is served in the dining room or out on the deck. You'll find plenty to do here during the day—tennis, swimming or just watching the wild ducks and geese swim in the pond. But if you want to venture into the adjacent redwood forests or down to the beach, the chefs will pack a picnic in a wicker basket or, for serious hikers, a knapsack lunch.

TIMBERHILL RANCH, 35755 Hauser Bridge Road, Cazadero, California 95421. Telephone: (707) 847-3458. Accommodations: ten cottages with queen-size beds; private baths with stall shower; one room with wheelchair access; no telephones; no television. Rates: very expensive, three meals included. Children and pets discouraged. Smoking and nonsmoking rooms. Cards: MC, VISA. Facilities for weddings if entire inn is booked Open all year.

Getting There: From Highway 1, about five miles north of Jenner, turn right onto Meyers Grade Road, which becomes Seaview. When you reach the turnoff to Plantation, swing right onto Hauser Bridge Road. The ranch is exactly 13.7 miles from Highway 1.

A Turreted Tribute to a Russian Past
ST. ORRES INN
Gualala

Turrets capped with onion-shaped domes frame this amazing architectural sculpture emblazened with leaded-glass windows and hand-carved balconies. Is this miniature palace overlooking the ocean a relic of the coast's Russian past? No: Eric Black, a carpenter of extraordinary skill and patience, built the inn in the 1970s on property that was once owned by the St. Orres family, who homesteaded the area. The inn is surrounded by forty-two acres of redwood-forested hillsides, where nine guest cottages now nestle.

When you enter the inn through a trellis-covered terrace, you can enjoy a glass of wine in a plant-filled solarium or beside the fire in a pretty parlor; oval windows offer peeks of the Pacific. Beyond is the spectacular dining room, where light filters down from stained-glass clerestories in the domed tower fifty feet above; three tiers of mullioned windows provide glimpses of forest and sea through a cascade of hanging plants.

St. Orres has one of the best restaurants on the entire north coast. Its menu changes seasonally, but you can usually count on rack of lamb with a Dijon mustard crust, a signature dish. Fresh local seafood is also featured, along with such entrées as medallions of venison and breast of duck. A complimentary breakfast of juices, fruit, house-baked breads and coffee is served here to inn guests. And on Sundays the public is welcome at an elaborate brunch.

Overnight accommodations vary widely from the small, inexpensive and rather spartan upstairs rooms in the main building to the delightful cottages hidden away in the redwoods. Some of these have fully equipped kitchens or wet bars; many have fireplaces or cast-iron stoves, private decks and ocean views. But everywhere you will find visual surprises—a skylight in an unexpected spot, handcrafted wood rafters or balustrades, or perhaps a bed on a raised platform, a sunken claw-footed bath or a Japanese soaking tub.

Three of the older cottages are sited beside a meadow behind the inn. The newer Creekside units, in a separate complex to the north, cluster around a turreted spa building that contains a hot tub, sauna, deck and kitchen facilities—an ideal spot for small conferences.

St. Orres Inn has its own private beach across the road. The area offers steelhead fishing in season, and weekend flea markets and arts and crafts festivals are popular events.

ST. ORRES INN, Highway 1 (P.O. Box 523), Gualala, California 95445. Telephone: (707) 884-3303. Accommodations: in the main building, eight rooms with double beds share three baths with showers; nine cottages with double or queen-size beds and private baths; no telephones; no television. Rates: inexpensive to expensive, Continental breakfast included. Dining room open to the public for dinner and Sunday brunch. Children welcome in cottages only. No pets. Cards: MC, VISA for overnight guests only; no credit cards accepted in dining room. Facilities for weddings and small conferences. Open all year.

Getting There: St. Orres Inn is located on Highway 1 between Gualala and Anchor Bay.

St. Orres Inn

WHALE WATCH INN BY THE SEA
Anchor Bay

Perched on sheer cliffs some fifty feet above the Pacific, this striking inn of contemporary design offers spectacular views of the ocean and the craggy coast. On this magnificent site, Irene and Enoch Stewart built a summer home in the 1970s, added some guest cottages, and by the 1980s their romantic inn had grown to eighteen rooms in a complex of five buildings.

Whale Watch, the original building, is now the central spot for those who want to socialize at the inn. It has a huge hexagonal living room paneled in redwood and glass with a freestanding fireplace in the center, its flue soaring up to the high pitched ceiling. A wide deck surrounds the ocean side, with stairways leading down to smaller decks with chairs for two—glorious spots to admire the view on sunny days. But even when rain or fog shroud the coast, this beautiful room provides a convivial spot to relax by the fire. There are plenty of comfortable couches, leather wing chairs, two game tables and a good assortment of books, puzzles, games and taped classical music. Several of the guest rooms are also in this building.

The four newer buildings are designed with privacy in mind. All have their own fireplaces, sitting areas, breakfast tables and decks to enjoy the view. If you wish, you need never see another person at Whale Watch, except the innkeepers when they bring around the breakfast trays laden with platters of fresh fruit, freshly baked bread and brie.

Pacific Edge, the newest building, offers the most luxurious accommodations, with skylights in the second-floor rooms and double or single whirlpool tubs throughout. One two-story suite provides the ultimate in a bathing experience: a spiral staircase ascends to a skylit room that has an enormous spa tub for two and an ocean view. In one of the older outbuildings, units have kitchens—fully equipped, down to cookbooks and herbs.

Wooden steps scale the perpendicular cliff below the Whale Watch Inn's flower-edged lawns, leading to a sandy sheltered beach. In winter and spring the favorite pastime here is watching the great gray whales swim by in their annual ten-thousand-mile migration between the arctic seas and the warm water off Baja California. February through April, when they return with their babies, are the best months to spot them.

WHALE WATCH INN BY THE SEA, 35100 Highway 1, Gualala, California 95445. Telephone: (707) 884-3667. Accommodations: eighteen rooms with twin or queen-size beds; private baths with tub/shower; no telephones; no television. Rates: expensive to very expensive, breakfast included. No children. No pets. No smoking. Cards: AE, MC, VISA. Open all year.

Getting There: The Whale Watch is on the ocean side of Highway 1 just north of Anchor Bay, which is five miles north of Gualala.

Edwardian Showplace from the Logging Era
HARBOR HOUSE
Elk

This stately house was built on the cliffs above Greenwood Landing by the Goodyear Redwood Lumber Company in 1916 to be used as an executive residence and for entertaining business guests. In those days the small port below was heavily trafficked by schooners coming for their rich cargoes of lumber from the nearby Albion forests. In fact the house itself is an enlarged replica of a redwood model house, designed by Louis Christian Mullgardt for the 1915 Pan American Exposition in San Francisco. When the lumber boom came to an end in the 1930s, Harbor House was converted to an inn.

The walls, vaulted ceiling and fireplace of the gracious living room are entirely paneled with hand-carved and hand-fitted redwood, still preserved by its original finish of polished hot beeswax. Furnishings are comfortable and eclectic: overstuffed chairs, a large Persian rug, a Steinway piano, Chinese chests and tables, bookcases bulging with reading matter, jigsaw puzzles and the like. In 1985 Helen and Dean Turner bought Harbor House from longtime innkeeper Patricia Corcoran. Except for adding some of their own antiques, they have kept the furnishings pretty much intact. They have also carried on Corcoran's tradition of providing substantial home-cooked meals, leisurely served in the dining room, where picture windows frame a view of the Pacific and the tunneled rocks in the harbor below.

A typical dinner, which is included in the room tariff, might start with a homemade tomato-basil soup, a salad of greens just picked from the inn's garden, a main course (often local lamb or seafood), homemade breads and maybe a fruit cobbler for dessert; guests may purchase wine from an extensive list of California bottlings. Breakfasts are bountiful,

209

too, focusing on a main course that might be spinach quiche, an oven-baked Gruyère omelet or perhaps a waffle made from freshly ground flour.

Six spacious bedrooms occupy the main house, five with fireplaces and one with a private deck. Many have ocean views and all are comfortably furnished in the style of an Edwardian country house. Next door, four cottages perch on the edge of the bluff; though small and somewhat rustic, these rooms do offer privacy, as well as ocean views.

Harbor House is only twenty minutes by car from Mendocino's shops and art galleries. But most guests choose to spend their time exploring the inn's private beach.

HARBOR HOUSE, P.O. Box 369, Elk, California 95432. Telephone: (707) 877-3203. Accommodations: nine rooms with twin, double or king-size beds; private baths with shower or tub/shower; no telephones; no television. Rates: expensive, full breakfast and dinner included. No children. No pets. No credit cards. Open all year.

Getting There: Harbor House is on the ocean side of Highway 1 just north of Elk, which is six miles south of the intersection of Highway 1 and Highway 128.

Where New England Meets the Wild West
MENDOCINO AREA

Cabrillo discovered Cape Mendocino in 1542 and named it after Don Antonio de Mendoza, first viceroy of New Spain. But except for its name, nothing about the coastal village of Mendocino is Spanish. Situated on a rocky bluff projecting into the Pacific, the town looks like a movie set of a New England village, reflecting the heritage of its founders. (In fact, a number of "New England" films have been shot here, including the TV series *Murder, She Wrote.*) Except for fresh paint, time has not touched the clapboard Victorians set among windmills, water towers and windswept cypress trees. Behind rise the redwood-covered mountains of the Coast Range.

It was this precious timber that attracted the early settlers to the Mendocino coast. Harry Meiggs, a San Francisco lumberman, brought the first sawmill to Mendocino from the East aboard the brig *Ontario*, and the lumber boom began. Others harvested the seafood from these northern waters and started a fishing industry that still flourishes in the nearby harbor of Noyo. In the late nineteenth century, some 3500 people lived in Mendocino, which then boasted eight hotels, seventeen saloons and as many bordellos.

Today the population is only eleven hundred and includes many artists and craftspeople. The entire town has been declared a historic monument so that its character will be preserved. Along Main Street, which faces the sea, and along picturesque side streets, where hollyhocks rise over picket fences, there are numerous art galleries and crafts shops. Within the area are tennis courts and a nine-hole golf course. The surrounding waters offer deep-sea and stream fishing, as well as canoeing.

Just north of Mendocino—but a continent away in atmosphere—is Fort Bragg, which looks like a typical western town and is still an active lumber center for the Georgia Pacific Company. Fort Bragg is also the departure point for the Skunk Train, which makes a scenic six-hour journey inland along the Noyo River through forty miles of redwoods. Advance reservations may be made by writing California Western Railroad, Box 907B, Fort Bragg, California 95437.

All along this coast, a favorite winter pastime is watching the migration of the great gray whales from the Arctic to Baja California and back. From December into April you can spot these thirty-ton mammals by the ten-foot water sprays they eject into the air. But the whale watch culminates during the last two weeks of March, when an annual whale festival is conducted in Mendocino and Fort Bragg. An even closer look is possible from charter boats operating out of the port of Noyo. Another favorite pastime—year-round—in this area is eating: a number of excellent restaurants dot the coast from Little River to Fort Bragg.

1860s Stagecoach Stop with a View

FENSALDEN INN
Albion

For over a century, this lovely house on a cypress-studded hillside overlooking the Pacific has been dispensing hospitality to north coast travelers. Built as a stagecoach way station in the 1860s, this hostelry, after an enormous amount of renovation, is now a bed and breakfast inn. The current owners, Scott and Frances Brazil, took it over in 1986 and have added improvements of their own, such as converting the old water tower into two attractive guest units.

In the main house, the spacious common room is particularly inviting, with a fireplace and a view of the sea through multipaned windows. A grand piano is well used: Frances is a professional pianist and former music professor at the University of Oklahoma. If you can coax her to the piano, you're in for a treat, but she says she doesn't play much anymore because she's so busy whipping up hors d'oeuvres and breakfasts for the guests.

The house contains four bedrooms with ocean or mountain views—or you can enjoy both these vistas from an upstairs suite that has a fireplace, too. The water-tower rooms also have fireplaces, as well as dramatic cathedral ceilings; one unit is actually a mini-apartment with a loft bedroom and a kitchenette. Actually, you need not worry about cooking at Fensalden Inn: it's only a short drive from the many good restaurants along the Mendocino coast.

FENSALDEN INN, Navarro Ridge Road (P.O. Box 99), Albion, California 95410. Telephone: (707) 937-4042. Accommodations: seven rooms and suites with queen- or king-size beds; private baths with shower or tub/shower; no telephones; no television. Rates: moderate to expensive, Continental breakfast included. Children over 12 welcome. No pets. No smoking. Cards: MC, VISA. Open all year.

Getting There: Just after Highway 128 joins Highway 1 (south of Albion), take Navarro Ridge Road east. The inn is on the left.

A Complex of Cottages above a Smugglers' Cove
HERITAGE HOUSE
Little River

In this ivy-covered inn with its many cottages rambling over hillsides, meadows and gardens reaching down to a private beach, L.D. Dennen and his daughter Gay strive to preserve the heritage of the Mendocino coast. Dennen's own roots are implanted in the history of the area. His grandfather, New Englander John Dennen, built the inn's main building as a home for rancher Wilder Pullen in 1876. During Prohibition, neighbors started to eye the former Pullen house with suspicion: Baby Face Nelson was using the cove below the house for his bootleg operations and, before his arrest, had concluded one of his last deals inside the house. As recently as the early 1940s, Chinese immigrants were smuggled into the country here.

Heritage House

In 1949 L.D. Dennen bought the house his grandfather had built and turned it into an inn. Over the years, he has added cottages on the meadows below the original house, building some and moving others from elsewhere in the countryside. All have names: Dennen built Schoolhouse with lumber salvaged from the Greenwood School in Elk; the school's sign serves as a headboard and the children's desks as bedside tables. Firehouse, Barbershop, Ice Cream are some other names. An old water tower, brought down from Mendocino, is now a two-story unit with a circular stairway leading from a living room to a balconied bedroom. There are now seventy units altogether, some with brick fireplaces or Franklin or pot-bellied stoves. All have private baths.

Some years back Dennen acquired an old apple storage house from a nearby farm for seventy-five dollars and rebuilt it next to the 1876 house as a bar. The comfortably furnished adjoining lounge with its walk-in fireplace commands magnificent views of the ocean. Even if you do not stay at Heritage House, you should at least drop by for a drink at sunset. The dining room also has wonderful views and is open to the public. The menu changes nightly: a typical dinner includes egg-lemon soup, greens mixed with pine nuts, Smithfield ham, a choice of grilled Pacific snapper with sauce mousseline or roast beef with sauce miroton along with fresh vegetables, fettuccine, and poppy-seed bread; and, as finale, a rich torte, fruit and cheese. Breakfasts, served on the deck on sunny days, are hearty too: a buffet of fruits, juices and cereals is followed by eggs Benedict (or any style), bacon, ham, sausage and dollar-size hotcakes. Heritage House operates on semi-American plan only; breakfast and dinner are included in the rates. This inn is more formal than most north coast places; jackets and ties are encouraged at dinner.

HERITAGE HOUSE, 5200 Highway 1, Little River, California 95456. Telephone: (707) 937-5885. Accommodations: seventy rooms with twin, double or king-size beds; private baths, some tub/shower, some shower only; rooms fully equipped for the handicapped; no telephones; no television. Rates: moderate to very expensive, breakfast and dinner included. Open to public for breakfast and dinner; full bar service. Children welcome. No pets. No credit cards. Open February through November.

Getting There: Heritage House is on the ocean side of Highway 1 between Albion and Little River.

214

THE STANFORD INN BY THE SEA
Mendocino

Just before you cross Big River on the way into the village of
Mendocino, you see a handsome lodge sitting on the hillside. Flowers
burst from its balconies, and manicured lawns and gardens slope down
to a pasture where llamas graze and ducks splash in a pond. This place,
also known as Big River Lodge, was built in the 1960s. In 1980 Joan and
Jeff Stanford transformed the motel-like structure into a lovely inn,
doing most of the work themselves.

Some of the rooms have walls of knotty pine or barn siding; all have
beamed ceilings, fireplaces and multipaned french doors leading to
private patios or balconies with magnificent ocean views. Each room is
individually decorated with antiques, four-posters, down quilts and the
like; coffee and other refreshments are there when you arrive.

The Stanfords' ten acres extend north to the wooded riverbank,
where a cottage contains three suites. There's a boat house here, too,
where you can rent canoes to paddle upstream or, in winter, to fish for
salmon and steelhead. Ten-speed and mountain bikes are also available
to explore the redwood forests behind the inn.

In the mornings, fruit, juices, hot Danish pastries, coffeecake and a
basket of fresh fruit are set out in the small lobby, but most guests
prefer to take their breakfasts back to their beautifully appointed
rooms. There's talk, however, of adding another building to house a
restaurant, which would make this a full-service inn.

THE STANFORD INN BY THE SEA (BIG RIVER LODGE),
Comptche-Ukiah Road (P.O. Box 487), Mendocino, California 95460.
Telephone: (707) 937-5615. Accommodations: twenty-five rooms and
three suites with queen- or king-size beds, some rooms with hide-a-
beds and trundle beds as well; private baths with stall shower or
tub/shower; wheelchair access; telephones; television. Rates: expensive
to very expensive, Continental breakfast included. Children and pets
welcome. Cards: AE, CB, DC, MC, VISA. Open all year.

Getting There: From Highway 1, just south of Mendocino, head east on
Comptche-Ukiah Road. The inn is on the left.

GLENDEVEN
Little River

This handsome New England-style farmhouse—flanked by two acres of cypress trees, lawns and flower gardens—stands on a headland overlooking the bay of Little River. Built in 1867 by Isaiah Stevens, an early settler from Maine, the house was acquired in 1977 by Dutch-born designer Jan de Vries and his wife Janet. They lavished improvements on it over the years, including a charming addition next door, until they now have one of the north coast's most distinguished inns.

The de Vrieses have skillfully decorated the rooms with a mix of good contemporary art and European antiques. Bright paintings, ceramics, prints and handmade quilts contrast with Louis XV bedsteads and marble-topped tables. The large living room is splashed with light from a bank of mullioned windows that look into the garden. In the evening, refreshments are served by the fireplace and, if you're lucky, a guest might play the baby grand. In the morning fresh fruit, juices and home-baked breads are served here or, if you like, in your room.

Accommodations in the farmhouse vary from two small rooms that share a bath to a suite with its own sitting room, fireplace and brick terrace. Atop the house, a garret room has skylights and a terrific view of the bay. The four units in the new building are more lavishly appointed; all have fireplaces and sitting areas, some have private decks or balconies, and the top-floor rooms have vaulted ceilings and skylights. But all of the rooms at Glendeven offer a vista of the gardens or meadow or bay.

GLENDEVEN, 8221 North Highway 1, Little River, California 95456. Telephone: (707) 937-0083. Accommodations: ten rooms with queen-size beds; all rooms have private baths except two, which share a bath; stall shower or tub/shower; no telephones; no television. Rates: moderate to expensive, Continental breakfast included. Children sometimes accepted. No pets. No smoking. Cards: MC, VISA by special arrangement. Open all year.

Getting There: Glendeven is north of Little River on the inland side of Highway 1.

Glendeven

A Testimonial to the Town's History
MENDOCINO HOTEL
Mendocino

The Old West facade of this historic hotel probably looks about the same as it did a century ago when Ben Bever started taking in lodgers here. Though it was once known as the Central Hotel, this landmark on Main Street has been the Mendocino Hotel as long as anyone can remember. But old Mendocino hands who have not been around in recent decades wouldn't recognize the present interior.

In 1973, San Diego businessman R. O. Peterson bought the hotel and renovated it to a level of luxury that had not existed before. Even in its prime, the hotel had been nothing fancy, just a comfortable hostelry for loggers and traveling salesmen. Peterson retained architect Wayne Williams and his wife Paula, an interior decorator, to invest the hotel with the elegance of the Victorian era. Polished dark woods and wainscotings, Oriental rugs and Tiffany-style glass were installed in the lobby and dining room. A spectacular dome of genuine Tiffany, found in Philadelphia, was suspended over the carved wooden bar. (Founder Bever surely wouldn't approve of the goings on today. He had once named the place The Temperance House, decreeing that "no liquor shall be served.") Off the lobby an attractive dining room is open to the public for dinner; breakfast and lunch are served in a plant-filled addition to the hotel.

Upstairs, twenty-six bedrooms have been renovated to mint condition. The decorator strived for an authentic, eclectic, turn-of-the-century ambience, combining hand-painted porcelain sinks from France and European armoires with replicated American wallpapers and Victorian brass and carved wooden beds. Many rooms have ocean views and private balconies.

Then, in the 1980s, Peterson nearly doubled the hostelry's capacity with four rear cottages, clustered around a formal garden in the block behind the hotel. One of these, now elegantly refurbished, was the home of the Heeser family, early settlers of the area. The other garden cottages, though newly constructed, also have the look of old Mendocino. The rooms in the cottages are more lavishly appointed than most of those in the hotel; many have wood-burning fireplaces or stoves, all have television and private bathrooms, and many have their own verandas. Each guest room is named after a pioneer Mendocino family, and yellowed photos of family members hang in the rooms, making you feel as though you're a part of the town's early history, too.

MENDOCINO HOTEL & GARDEN COTTAGES, 45080 Main Street (P.O. Box 587), Mendocino, California 95460. Telephone: (707) 937-0511, in California (800) 352-6686, nationwide (800) 421-6662. Accommodations: fifty-one rooms and suites with twin, double, two double, queen- or king-size beds; most rooms have private baths with tub/shower; in the hotel some have shared baths with stall shower; some rooms fully equipped for the handicapped; no telephones; television in garden cottages. Rates: moderate to very expensive, no meals included. Dining room open to the public for breakfast, lunch and dinner; full bar service. Children welcome. No pets. Cards: AE, MC, VISA. Facilities for conferences. Open all year.

Getting There: From Highway 1, turn left at the Mendocino exit onto Jackson Street, which becomes Main Street.

Lively New Life for an Older Inn
MENDOCINO VILLAGE INN
Mendocino

When you enter the village of Mendocino, one of the first sights you see, behind a pretty garden and a white picket fence, is the Mendocino Village Inn. If you've been here before, you might do a double-take after a glimpse of the well-manicured grounds and the sparkling paint job on the 1882 Queen Anne Victorian. Sue and Tom Allen bought the place in 1986 and gave it a sorely needed face-lift and an entire new life.

The interior has been spruced up, too, and furnished with eclectic abandon. Some rooms have a traditional look with flowered papers and old four-posters, while others are decked out with Navajo rugs and Indian art. Then there are the Captain's Quarters, with nautical memorabilia, and the Roosevelt Room, with trophies that might have been Teddy's. Many of the rooms have wood-burning fireplaces, others have views, and a few have private garden entrances. Two inexpensive garret rooms occupy the top floor—a perfect spot for older children or young budget travelers who might not mind sharing a bath located down a steep flight of stairs.

The Allens are engaging hosts and have interesting backgrounds. They have lived in New York, Japan and San Francisco, where she managed an architectural office and he was in advertising. They have made the homey first-floor common room the hub of the inn, joining their guests in the evening for refreshments and lively discussions of

219

politics or the arts. They serve a hearty breakfast: fresh fruit, homemade breads and main dishes the likes of herbed cheesecake or blue-cornmeal pancakes. There are large tables, if you feel sociable, as well as tiny tables for two. Or if you like, take your coffee out to the redwood deck and listen to the taped music that's an integral part of a stay here. In the morning it's classical and in the evening it's jazz— perhaps Brubeck, the Manhattan Transfer or Jean-Luc Ponty. If the tapes run out don't worry: this place has a guitar and a piano, too.

MENDOCINO VILLAGE INN, Main Street (P.O. Box 626), Mendocino, California 95460. Telephone: (707) 937-0246. Accommodations: twelve rooms with double and queen-size beds; all have private baths except two, which share a bath; tub, stall shower or tub/shower; no telephones; no television. Rates: inexpensive to moderate, breakfast included. Children welcome in some rooms. No pets. No smoking. Cards: MC, VISA. Open all year.

Getting There: At Mendocino, exit from Highway 1 onto Jackson Street, which becomes Main Street.

A Fireplace and Flowers in Every Room
HEADLANDS INN
Mendocino

Of the many north coast inns that have opened in the 1980s, Headlands is one of the loveliest. The three-story, nineteenth-century shingled house, surrounded by a picket fence and a flower-filled garden, commands unobstructed views of the Big River inlet and the tree-covered mountains beyond. Rich champagne-colored carpeting flows throughout the rooms, which are painted and papered in restful tones of beige and white and furnished with English and American antiques. All rooms have wood-burning fireplaces, most have ocean views, and one has dutch doors leading to a private deck. All are appointed with comfortable couches and chairs, queen- or king-size beds, magazines, plants and flowers—even in the spacious private baths.

In 1986 former San Franciscans Pat and Rod Stofle purchased Headlands and added a few improvements of their own. Most noticeably, they turned the first-floor bedroom into a gracious parlor with a fireplace and an antique piano. A second-floor common room remains, with games, books and even a drafting table for would-be artists.

Breakfast is still brought to your room on a tray with the morning paper, but the Stofles plan to add a dining area next to the parlor. Pat loves to cook, and in addition to freshly baked breads, fresh fruit and juice, she prepares a special entrée each day. This might be a Florentine ham roll with a cheddar cheese sauce or an individual Mexican soufflé with salsa or a baked apple stuffed with a cranberry-sausage filling. "I don't paint or sew," she says. "Cooking is my way of being creative."

HEADLANDS INN, 44950 Albion Street (P.O. Box 132), Mendocino, California 95460. Telephone: (707) 937-4431. Accommodations: five rooms with queen- or king-size beds; private baths with tub/shower; no telephones; no television. Rates: moderate to expensive, breakfast included. No children. No pets. No credit cards. No smoking. Open all year.

Getting There: Take Jackson Street exit off Highway 1. Turn right on Howard Street to Albion Street. The inn is on the corner.

JOSHUA GRINDLE INN
Mendocino

Joshua Grindle came to Mendocino from Maine in the 1860s and had become the town banker by 1879, when he built a fine house overlooking the village and the ocean. In 1977 Bill and Gwen Jacobson, who had been searching the state for a B&B site, bought the house, its imposing water tower and the surrounding two acres. In keeping with Grindle's New England heritage, they decorated the rooms with Early American furnishings, many from their own collection of eighteenth- and nineteenth-century antiques.

On the first floor, one bedroom is papered with historic scenes of Philadelphia, boasts a handsome maple four-poster, and overlooks a patio shaded by a giant rhododendron tree. Another is decorated with pale yellow woodwork, a peony-patterned quilt on a queen-size bed, and comfortable chairs around a fireplace. An upstairs room has a nautical theme and a fine ocean view. Joshua Grindle's former bedroom, with its dormered windows, is large enough for three, with a queen-size bed and a studio couch. An adjacent saltbox cottage contains two rooms with Franklin stoves, and the water tower has been remodeled to create another three units, two with fireplaces.

Yet another fireplace, decorated with hand-painted English tiles distinguishes the paneled living room. A baby grand piano is also there for the guests' enjoyment, as are jigsaw puzzles, backgammon and chess sets. In the cheerful dining room an antique pine refectory table, a handsome old hutch and a grandmother's clock catch the eye. Here Gwen serves a full breakfast of homemade bread or coffeecake, fresh fruits, eggs, coffee and tea. The Jacobsons will be happy to brief you on activities in the area, but if you want to be left alone, they won't intrude. That's one of the reasons travelers return again and again to this exemplary inn.

JOSHUA GRINDLE INN, 44800 Little Lake, Mendocino, California 95460. Telephone: (606) 937-4143. Accommodations: ten rooms with double or queen-size beds; private baths with tub/shower; no telephones; no television; one room with wheelchair access. Rates: moderate, full breakfast included. No children. No pets. No smoking. No credit cards. Open all year.

Getting There: From Highway 1, take Jackson Street exit into Mendocino. Turn right on Lansing to Little Lake.

Joshua Grindle Inn

Only a Few Clues to an Unusual Past
THE GREY WHALE INN
Fort Bragg

When John and Collette Bailey bought this three-story building on Fort Bragg's Main Street in 1974, they started a massive remodeling program. Carpeting and private baths were added and the rooms were decorated with comfortable, homey furnishings, quilted bedspreads with matching linens, and paintings by local artists. One would never guess the inn's unusual past: it functioned as a hospital for some sixty years. But a few clues do remain, such as an old examining table in the second-floor lounge, extra-wide doors, a window in the door of the former nursery and an overhead surgery lamp in one of the suites.

Some of the fourteen rooms have natural redwood or pecky cedar paneling; some have ocean views; one has a fireplace; another has an interior patio. Two glassed-in penthouse rooms have private decks and views of the ocean or mountains. Books and magazines abound in the bedrooms and in a small first-floor sitting room, where the Baileys have thoughtfully provided scrapbooks of information on local attractions, restaurants and other inns throughout California. There's also a recreation room with a billiard table and TV set.

In the morning, guests are treated to Collette's prize-winning baked goods. She has won six blue ribbons at the Mendocino County Fair for the breads and coffeecakes served at the inn. These are set out in a buffet breakfast that includes a selection of fresh fruits and juices, yogurt, cheese, or egg casseroles. It's a repast guaranteed to provide vigor for an activity-filled day.

GREY WHALE INN, 615 North Main Street, Fort Bragg, California 95437. Telephone: (707) 964-0640; in California (800) 382-7244. Accommodations: fourteen rooms with twin, double, queen- or king-size beds; private baths; some kitchens; no telephones; no television; wheelchair access. Rates: inexpensive to moderate, breakfast included. Children over 12 welcome. No pets. Cards: AE, MC, VISA. Open all year.

1884 Residence of a Russian Count

PUDDING CREEK INN
Fort Bragg

Fort Bragg's Main Street should be renamed Bed and Breakfast Boulevard for the many B&Bs that have appeared on it in the last few years. One of the nicest is Gene and Marilyn Gundersen's Pudding Creek Inn, which, along with their country store, occupies two century-old houses connected by an enclosed garden. The houses supposedly were built by a Russian count, and in his honor the Gundersens display in the parlor the countess' wedding gown, a photograph of the titled pair and other memorabilia they found in the buildings. The parlor also serves as a breakfast room for a morning repast of fresh fruits and juices, homemade coffeecake and more. But most guests prefer to be served in the cheerful old-fashioned kitchen or in the garden, which is a veritable jungle of hanging begonias, fuschias and ferns. Water splashes from a little fountain here and, weather permitting, refreshments are served here in the evening.

The Gundersens have decorated the bedrooms with country and Victorian furnishings, flowered wallpapers and quilted spreads. One of the rooms, named after the count, is paneled with inlaid redwood and has a large stone fireplace, another has a brick fireplace and a third has its own sitting room. But each room in the inn also has its individual touch: an antique spinning wheel in one, a school desk for a nightstand in another, and a window box filled with pelargoniums in yet another.

PUDDING CREEK INN, 700 North Main Street, Fort Bragg, California 95437. Telephone: (707) 964-9529. Accommodations: ten rooms with twin, double, queen- or king-size beds; private baths with tub or shower; no telephones; no television. Rates: inexpensive to moderate, Continental breakfast included. Children over 10 welcome. No pets. No smoking, except in garden. Cards: MC, VISA. Open all year.

A Great Place to Do Nothing

THE TOLL HOUSE INN
Boonville

Midway between Elk and Mendocino, Highway 128 heads inland, following the Navarro River through dense redwood groves, then through vineyards and orchards to the little town of Boonville. From here Highway 253 twists over the mountains to Ukiah through hilly pastures which have been sheep grazing territory for over a century. In 1912, one of the pioneer sheep-ranching families, the Millers, built a house six miles up this road from Boonville. At that time they maintained the road and charged a toll to the loggers who hauled their redwood along this route to inland mills.

In 1981 Beverly Nesbitt bought the place to establish it as a home and inn. And a gracious and restful home it is. Two pillowy couches by the fireplace invite you to relax in the lovely living room, where multipaned windows open to the gardens beyond. Here you have your choice of lazing in a hammock on a shady veranda, sunning on a secluded wooden deck or sun porch. Or, if you want privacy, you can curl up on the comfortable daybed in your room—and two of the rooms have fireplaces. Beverly has decorated the rooms in a riot of floral prints on the wallpapers, curtains, bedspreads and linens.

A day at the Toll House begins with a big country breakfast in the dining room overlooking the gardens. There's usually fresh-squeezed orange juice and sometimes apples from the inn's old orchard, followed by whatever Beverly feels like cooking: omelets, oatmeal and corn muffins, pancakes or waffles. For guests who make arrangements in advance, dinners are served here too. If you're a twosome, she whips up a casual three-course supper, but for larger groups, it's a feast beginning with appetizers like Greek spanakopeta, followed by soup, entrée (often local lamb), vegetables, salad and a homemade pastry.

The Toll House's remote setting attracts those who want to get away from activity. "It's the greatest do-nothing inn in the world," Bev proclaims. Then again, it's only a twenty-minute drive to Ukiah's fine wineries, such as Parducci and Fetzer, and only ten minutes to the wineries of Boonville.

THE TOLL HOUSE INN, 15301 Highway 253 (P.O. Box 268), Boonville, California 95415. Telephone: (707) 895-3630. Accommodations; three rooms with queen-size bed and daybed plus one room with Murphy bed; two rooms with private bath, two rooms share bath with tub and shower; wheelchair access; telephone upon request in one room; television in solarium. Rates: moderate to expensive, breakfast included. No children under 10. No pets. No smoking. No credit cards. Open all year.

Getting There: From San Francisco take Highway 101 to Cloverdale, Highway 128 west to Boonville and Highway 253 northeast toward Ukiah. The inn is about six miles up this highway.

The Empress of the Redwood Empire
BENBOW INN
Garberville

In 1926 the Benbow family commissioned San Francisco architect Albert Farr to design a small luxury hotel on the banks of the Eel River in a remote valley surrounded by forests of giant redwoods. Farr created a four-story English Tudor manor house of half-timbered construction—an incongruous sight in this mountain setting. The baronial lobby—with its high, coffered ceiling, carved woodwork, massive fireplace of sculptured stone, and french doors leading to a formal terrace—was a gathering place for the elite of the era. John Barrymore, Charles Laughton, President Hoover and Mrs. Eleanor Roosevelt were among Benbow's early guests. But even they would be astounded at the luxuriance of the Benbow today.

In the 1940s this fine old inn slid into a period of genteel shabbiness, despite efforts at improvement by a string of owners. Nostalgia was almost all it had going for it in 1978 when Patsy and Chuck Watts rescued the aging dowager and transformed it into the empress of the Redwood Empire. Now the lobby is resplendent with carved period furniture, Oriental rugs and an impressive array of antique clocks, paintings and prints, which are found throughout the inn as well. The terrace and gardens are a blaze of color from over three dozen varieties of flowering plants. Upstairs, the Wattses installed carved cherry paneling in the hallways and thick carpeting throughout, and all the bedrooms now have modern tiled bathrooms and a lovely country look, with matching floral bedspreads, draperies and wallpaper. A coffeepot and a basket of paperback mysteries are provided with the inn's compliments. In the deluxe rooms, small refrigerators are stocked with beverages.

The second- and third-story rooms of the Benbow have views of the surrounding terrain from large windows or bays. These used to be the choice rooms, but that distinction now belongs to two stories of rooms under the terrace overlooking the river. These once were the bane of Benbow, but in 1983 Patsy and Chuck rebuilt them from the ground up, adding all the accoutrements of the upstairs rooms, plus wood-burning fireplaces in some and private terraces or balconies adjacent to all. A rebuilt cottage offers a Jacuzzi as well.

Despite Benbow's isolation, there's no lack of things to do. The dining room is one of the finest restaurants in the Redwood Empire, with a sophisticated menu featuring the likes of Provimi milk-fed veal

Benbow Inn

with a Dijon mustard sauce or Long Island duckling embellished with apricots and Grand Marnier. A jukebox is filled with big-band favorites—Glenn Miller, Freddy Martin, Artie Shaw, etc.—and a piano player entertains nightly in the lounge just off the lobby. In another salon, old-time movies from a library of some one hundred classic films are shown each night. And there's always the possibility of a game of chess or a jigsaw puzzle in the lobby. The Watts also stage special events at certain times of the year: a Halloween masquerade ball, a November tasting of Napa Valley wines, a nutcracker Christmas celebration and a New Year's Eve champagne dinner-dance.

A plethora of daytime activities is available as well: In the summer the Eel river is dammed into a lake, offering swimming from the inn's private beach, canoeing and paddleboating. Nearby are tennis courts, a nine-hole golf course, fishing, hunting and horseback-riding trails. Seven miles south of Benbow is Richardson Grove State Park, one of California's most important redwood preserves, and to the north is the Avenue of the Giants, a road that winds through dense groves of sequoias, the world's largest, oldest trees.

BENBOW INN, 445 Lake Benbow Drive, Garberville, California 95440. Telephone: (707) 923-2124. Accommodations: fifty-six rooms with twin, queen- or king-size beds; private baths; no telephones; color television in terrace rooms; central air conditioning. Rates: moderate to very expensive, no meals included. Dining room open to the public for breakfast, lunch, dinner and Sunday brunch; full bar service. Children over three welcome. Dogs allowed. Credit cards: MC, VISA. Open April 1 to December 1, and December 18 through January 2.

Getting There: Benbow Inn is 200 miles north of San Francisco, two miles south of Garberville, on Highway 101. From the Mendocino coast, Benbow may be reached by taking Highway 1 to Leggett and then north on 101. The inn will send a car to Garberville airport for guests arriving by private plane.

A Mecca for Lovers of Victorian Architecture
EUREKA AND FERNDALE

Eureka shares its name with California's motto: I have found it! It wasn't gold that the city's founders had discovered in 1850, but rather a large bay at the mouth of the Eel River. This was a convenient harbor for ships awaiting a cargo almost as precious as gold: the redwood hewn in the great sequoia groves through which the Eel flows. Ferndale's first settlers were not seeking gold either; they were dairy farmers attracted by the verdant pastureland along the river's broad delta. Today, however, visitors are lured to this area by another kind of treasure: both Eureka and Ferndale are gold mines of well-preserved Victorian architecture.

The county seat, Eureka is the largest port north of San Francisco and a bustling commercial center for the lumber and fishing industries, which are still thriving. Yet the city is preserving its heritage in Old Eureka, a re-creation of the old town along the waterfront. Ferndale, on the other hand, remains a sleepy community that has changed little since the nineteenth century. Its Main Street is lined with brightly painted Victorian buildings that now house a bevy of shops, arts and crafts galleries, restaurants and the Village Theatre, home of the Ferndale Repertory Company. The entire town has been designated an historical landmark by the state of California and has been dubbed "the Victorian Village."

The drive to this area follows the Eel River from the redwood-forested mountains down to the sea. Beyond Garberville you will see a number of turnoffs to the Avenue of the Giants. This is the old road that winds through the dense groves of sequoias, some of which are over three thousand years old and as tall as 350 feet. It's worth the detour for the awesome experience of being among some of the world's oldest living things.

Getting There: Eureka is 277 miles north of San Francisco on Highway 101. The turnoff to Ferndale is clearly marked shortly before the highway reaches Eureka.

As Flamboyant as a Victorian Can Be

THE GINGERBREAD MANSION
Ferndale

Every architectural gewgaw known in the 1890s was lavished on this showplace: its gables and turrets were festooned with intricately carved spoolwork, brackets, finials and friezes and painted in flamboyant tones of peach and gold. Flanked by a formal English garden where brick walkways lead through a maze of manicured boxwoods and topiaries, The Gingerbread Mansion makes a stunning sight on this quiet side street of Ferndale. The same Victorian spirit pervades the inside of the house. The rooms are papered with colorful replicas of Victorian patterns and furnished with period pieces—an Empire couch and Eastlake parlor set in the living room, a Hoosier hutch in the adjoining library with an abundant supply of books, games and puzzles, and carved headboards in the upstairs bedrooms.

Ever since they acquired the house in 1981, innkeepers Wendy Hatfield and Ken Torbet have continually improved it. Five of the eight bedrooms now have private baths, and the Gingerbread Suite also has two old-fashioned claw-legged tubs right in the bedroom; bubble bath and tubside reading lamps are provided. But even guests who share baths are not deprived: The most popular room in the house, according to Wendy, is the two-hundred-square-foot bathroom where a huge claw-legged tub sits in splendor on a raised platform surrounded by a white rail fence. Green and pink irises on the French wallpaper, a matching stained glass window, hanging plants, a mirrored ceiling and a bidet complete the picture.

Wendy, who was formerly in the travel business, treats her guests with a hospitality as lavish as the gingerbread facade of the house. Late afternoon tea and cake are served at fireside in the inn's four parlors, beds are turned down at night and a hand-dipped chocolate is placed on the bedside table. In the morning trays of coffee and tea are set out upstairs so guests can have an eye-opener before proceeding to the formal dining room for a breakfast of fruits, cheeses and homemade muffins, breads and cakes. The inn even provides high boots for rainy days and bicycles to explore the town. These are painted the same gold and peach as the house, so the shopkeepers can recognize guests from The Gingerbread Mansion.

THE GINGERBREAD MANSION, 400 Berding Street, Ferndale, California 95536. Telephone: (707) 786-4000. Accommodations: eight

The Gingerbread Mansion

rooms with twin, double and queen-size beds; five private baths and two shared baths with tub and shower; no telephones; no television. Rates: moderate, Continental breakfast included. No children under 10. No pets. No smoking. Cards: MC, VISA. Open all year.

Southern Hospitality in a Gothic Mansion
THE SHAW HOUSE INN
Ferndale

In the early 1850s, Seth Shaw and his brother Stephen were the first settlers of the rich farmlands south of the Eel River, replacing jungles of twelve-foot-high ferns with orchards and cultivated fields. Seth chose a spot on the banks of Francis Creek to erect a gabled carpenter gothic mansion for his bride and named the estate Fern Dale. But as other farmers populated the area, the town name was contracted to Ferndale. As late as 1980, when most of the other Victorians in the town had been restored to mint condition, the old Shaw house remained empty and neglected, its acre of wooded grounds overgrown with weeds and ferns. Then Velna Polizzi, a native of North Carolina, took over. She renovated the house, moved in her enormous collections of antique furnishings, classic and contemporary paintings, rare china and porcelain, and books, numbering in the thousands, on almost every subject. Then she opened her doors to overnight guests, offering the generous hospitality for which Southerners are known.

As you open the gate to the garden, it's likely you'll be welcomed by Amber, Velna's gregarious cat, who will follow you to the library, where Velna might offer you a cup of tea by the fireside. The mansion itself is distinguished by an abundance of bays and coffered ceilings—even under the sloping roof of the second-story gables—and there is a deck overlooking Francis Creek off the dining room. Four of the guest rooms are located upstairs. Two of them have Gothic doors opening to private balconies, and a third holds the Shaws' honeymoon bed with its handsome six-foot headboard. Another bedroom is reached through double doors off the downstairs parlor. All of the guest rooms have homelike touches: potpourri, fresh flowers and fruit, dishes of mints, pincushions, music boxes and whatnot.

In the morning Velna sets the Empire table in the formal dining room with sterling silver and pieces of Delft, Chinese and English china for a breakfast that includes fruit compote, hot bread and an entrée such as quiche or whatever else she is inspired to cook. Throughout a

The Shaw House Inn

stay at Shaw House, Velna will overwhelm you with suggestions on what to do and see in and around Ferndale. If her soft southern accent didn't belie it, you'd think she was a native, she's so well versed in the history of the area.

THE SHAW HOUSE INN, 703 Main Street, Ferndale, California 95536. Telephone: (707) 786-9958. Accommodations: five rooms with twin, double or queen-size beds; two private half baths, one shared bath with tub; no telephones; no television. Rates: moderate, full breakfast included. No small children. No pets. No smoking. No credit cards. Open all year.

Handcrafted Victorian Circa 1980
CARTER HOUSE
Eureka

Samuel and Joseph C. Newsom, architects of Eureka's famous Carson Mansion, also designed a number of other buildings in the city. One of their admirers is Mark Carter, the son of a local real estate developer, who had helped renovate some Newsom structures owned by his father. When he found an old book of Newsom house plans, he decided to build one from scratch. The design he chose had been built in 1884 for a San Francisco banker named Murphy on the corner of Bush and Jones but was destroyed in the 1906 fire. Now Mark has faithfully re-created it on a hillside in Eureka—a stunning Victorian that offers views of the bay and of the nearby Carson Mansion from almost every room.

Mark and a carpenter friend, along with two helpers, built the four-story structure themselves, handcrafting the intricate detailings on the wood wainscotings and moldings. "The only old things we used," he confesses, "are a pair of brass hinges and two sinks." They followed the Newsom plans in every respect with only one deviation, a bay window in the entry that splashes the hallway with light. In fact, unlike most Victorians, the entire house has a light and airy feeling of flowing space. Joseph Newsom himself wrote, "The lower portion of the house can be thrown open to form a very fine continuous room." And so it is today with the three parlors distinguished by two marble fireplaces and three large bays. Mark did depart, however, from the Victorian tradition of interior design by painting the walls a stark white and eliminating the frills and clutter associated with the period. The decor is beautifully

Carter House

understated, with well-chosen and well-placed antiques, Oriental rugs scattered on the highly polished oak floors, no curtains or drapes to shut out the light, contemporary paintings and ceramics by local artists, and baskets of flowers and potted plants strategically set about.

Three guest rooms with high-pitched ceilings occupy the top floor; the other two, as well as the wine cellar, are located at street level on a floor below the parlor. The third floor contains another guest room and a two-room suite with a whirlpool bath for two.

Christi is an avid cook. One of her breakfast specialties is a recipe learned in classes with Jacques Pepin: a delicate tart with a ground almond filling topped by very thin slices of apple. This might be accompanied with fresh orange juice, eggs Florentine or Benedict or a smoked salmon platter, and a fruit dish such as kiwi with puréed raspberries or zabaglione with fresh strawberries. In the late afternoon the Carters serve brie and fruit, and at bedtime they offer tea and cookies. For groups who take over the entire inn, Mark and Christi will prepare sit-down, seven-course dinners.

CARTER HOUSE, Third and L streets, Eureka, California 95501. Telephone: (707) 445-1390. Accommodations: seven rooms with double, two double or queen-size beds; one room fully equipped for the handicapped; four rooms with private baths, three rooms share a bath with tub/shower; no telephones; no television. Rates: inexpensive to very expensive, breakfast included. No children. No pets. No smoking in bedrooms. Cards: AE, MC, VISA. Open all year.

Getting There: From the south, Highway 101 becomes Fifth Street. Turn left on L Street for two blocks.

Re-Creation of a Victorian Hotel
THE CARTER HOTEL
Eureka

Mark Carter might wind up rebuilding Eureka if he keeps up his whirlwind pace of reconstructing Victorians. After turning The Carter House B&B (see preceding) into a smashing success, he built a hotel across the street, modeled after Eureka's Old Town Cairo Hotel. Working from an old photograph, he constructed a three-story Queen Anne–type building with a gabled roof, twenty bedrooms, wide hallways and an enormous lobby.

The Carter Hotel is oriented toward the business traveler. The rooms, furnished with antique pine, offer modern comforts such as private baths (some with whirlpool tubs), television and telephones. Two rooms have fireplaces, too. Like The Carter House, the hotel reflects Mark's passion for contemporary art, which is found throughout the place. The Carter Hotel also offers fine views of Humboldt Bay. Guests have the option here of choosing a B&B plan, in which a Continental breakfast is included in the rate.

CARTER HOTEL, 301 L Street, Eureka, California 95501. Telephone: (707) 445-1490. Accommodations: twenty rooms with two double or queen-size beds; private baths, six with whirlpool tubs; telephones; television. Rates: moderate, with or without breakfast. Children welcome. No pets. No smoking in guest rooms. Cards: AE, MC, VISA. Facilities for weddings. Open all year.

Getting There: See directions to The Carter House, preceding.

INDEX

INDEX TO LOCATIONS

CHILDREN UNDER 12 WELCOME
Sometimes subject to certain restrictions; see listing.

Mendocino Village Inn, Mendocino, 219–220
St. Orres Inn, Gualala, 205–207
Stanford Inn by the Sea, Mendocino, 215

PETS WELCOME
Sometimes subject to certain restrictions; see listing.

SOUTHERN CALIFORNIA
Inn at Rancho Santa Fe, Rancho Santa Fe, 12–14
San Ysidro Ranch, Montecito, 28–31
GOLD COUNTRY
National Hotel, Jamestown, 155–156
WINE COUNTRY
Auberge du Soleil, Rutherford, 179
Madrona Manor, Healdsburg, 192–194
Vintners Inn, Santa Rosa, 197–198
REDWOOD EMPIRE
Benbow Inn, Garberville, 228–230
Stanford Inn by the Sea, Mendocino, 215

SWIMMING POOLS

SOUTHERN CALIFORNIA
El Encanto Hotel, Santa Barbara, 34–36
Inn at Rancho Santa Fe, Rancho Santa Fe, 12–14
San Ysidro Ranch, Montecito, 28–31
Seal Beach Inn & Gardens, Seal Beach, 15–16
Union Hotel, Los Alamos, 47–48
Villa Rosa, Santa Barbara, 36–37
CENTRAL COAST
Highlands Inn, Carmel Highlands, 80–81
Inn at Morro Bay, Morro Bay, 54
Quail Lodge, Carmel Valley, 78–79
Ventana Inn, Big Sur, 57–58
GOLD COUNTRY
Gate House Inn, Jackson, 148–150
Mine House, Amador City, 141–142
WINE COUNTRY
Auberge du Soleil, Rutherford, 179
Hope-Bosworth House, Geyserville, 189–191
Hope-Merrill House, Geyserville, 189–191
Madrona Manor, Healdsburg, 192–194
Magnolia Hotel, Yountville, 176–178
Meadowood, St. Helena, 184
Victorian Garden Inn, Sonoma, 172–173
Wine Country Inn, St. Helena, 182–183
REDWOOD EMPIRE
Timberhill Ranch, Timber Cove Ridge, 204–205

TENNIS

SOUTHERN CALIFORNIA
El Encanto Hotel, Santa Barbara, 34–36
Inn at Rancho Santa Fe, Rancho Santa Fe, 12–14
San Ysidro Ranch, Montecito, 28–31
CENTRAL COAST
Highlands Inn, Carmel Highlands, 80–81
WINE COUNTRY
Auberge du Soleil, Rutherford, 179
Meadowood, St. Helena, 184
REDWOOD EMPIRE
Timberhill Ranch, Timber Cove Ridge, 204–205

GOLF

CENTRAL COAST
Quail Lodge, Carmel Valley, 78–79
WINE COUNTRY
Meadowood, St. Helena, 184

RESTAURANTS

SOUTHERN CALIFORNIA
El Encanto Hotel, Santa Barbara, 34–36
Inn at Rancho Santa Fe, Rancho Santa Fe, 12–14
Rose Victorian Inn, Arroyo Grande, 49–50
San Ysidro Ranch, Montecito, 28–31
Union Hotel, Los Alamos, 47–48
Upham, Santa Barbara, 31–33
CENTRAL COAST
Highlands Inn, Carmel Highlands, 80–81
Inn at Morro Bay, Morro Bay, 54
Quail Lodge, Carmel Valley, 78–79
Ventana Inn, Big Sur, 57–58
SAN FRANCISCO BAY AREA
Casa Madrona Hotel, Sausalito, 115–117
Garden Court Hotel, Palo Alto, 114
Union Hotel, Benicia, 128
GOLD COUNTRY
City Hotel, Columbia, 152–154
Jamestown Hotel, Jamestown, 156–158
National Hotel, Jamestown, 155–156
WINE COUNTRY
Auberge du Soleil, Rutherford, 179
Madrona Manor, Healdsburg, 192–194
Meadowood, St. Helena, 184
Sonoma Hotel, Sonoma, 170–171
Vintners Inn, Santa Rosa, 197–198
REDWOOD EMPRIE
Benbow Inn, Garberville, 228–230

PRIVATE WHIRLPOOLS

KITCHEN FACILITIES
Sometimes only in a few units.

TERRIFIC VIEWS
From a number of rooms.

FACILITIES FOR THE HANDICAPPED

The following inns have complete facilities, such as fully equipped baths. Many others have wheelchair access to some rooms.

101 COUNTRY INNS BOOKS

Country Inns of the Far West: California (1987) $8.95
Country Inns of the Far West: Pacific Northwest (1987) $8.95
Country Inns of the Great Lakes (1987) $8.95
Country Inns of the Mid Atlantic (1986) $7.95
Country Inns of New England (1987) $8.95
Country Inns of New York (1985) $7.95
Country Inns of the Southwest (1985) $7.95
Country Inns of Texas (1987) $8.95
Country Inns Cookery $7.95
Bread & Breakfast $7.95
So You Want to Be an Innkeeper $10.95

If you cannot find these books in your local bookstore,
they may be ordered from the publisher:
101 Productions, 834 Mission Street, San Francisco CA 94103
Please add $1.00 per copy for postage and handling.
California residents add sales tax.

TO ORDER: Indicate quantity for each title above and fill in form below.
Send with check or money order to 101 Productions.

NAME _____

ADDRESS _____

CITY_____ STATE_____ ZIP_____

JACQUELINE KILLEEN is a fourth-generation Californian who has been traveling around the state since the 1930s and writing about it since 1968, when her first book *101 Nights in California* was published. She is also co-author of *Best Restaurants/San Francisco Bay Area* and of *Country Inns Cookery,* as well as another cookbook, *101 Secrets of California Chefs.* She is a restaurant critic for *San Francisco Focus* magazine and contributor to the restaurant section of *Fodor's San Francisco* and has written articles on California for a number of national magazines.

ROY KILLEEN, an architect, contributed not only the drawings for this book but also much technical advice about furnishings and the style of the buildings. He was formerly a project architect with Anshen and Allen of San Francisco and, like many of the innkeepers, has renovated a number of Victorian buildings. He also has designed 101 Productions' Mini-Mansion® series of historical architectural models and illustrated a number of 101 books.